Good Thyme
Herb Blends Cookbook

A User's Guide

by DEBRA DAWSON

Recipes, tips and techniques for using
Good Thyme Herb Blends

A Fresh Look At Seasoning

Drawn from years of hard work and good food
in catering and fine restaurants on the
Mendocino Coast of California

Copyright © 1993 by

Debra Dawson

Good Thyme Press
Post Office Box 975
Mendocino, California 95460

First Printing 1993
Printed in the United States of America

ISBN # 0-9635515-1-5

Acknowledgments

Arrigo D'Albert, my partner and critic, who sure can eat. Thanks for keeping the standards high.

Jacques Péré, who introduced me to food, my teacher.

Monique Frankston and **Fabia D'Albert**—if either of them is cooking, I'll be there.

Grail Dawson—my Dad—and **Betty Barber**, for support, advice and consent. And if Betty's cooking, I'll be *there*, too.

Linda Friedman and everyone at the *Chocolate Moosse Café*— who served all my soups, no matter how odd.

Penny and G.F. Cloud of *Clouds' Pottery*, **Lousia Carter** of *Lousia's Mustard*, and **Carol Hall** of the *Hot Pepper Jelly Company*—for advice, encouragement, and showing the way.

Kathi Edwards at *Computer Solution* for patience, integrity, and assistance at every step, forward and backward. **Sonya Roberts** for finding the time to type the first draft. **Ronnie James** and **Holly Tannen** for editing and proof-reading at just the right moments.

Mickie Zekeley of *Lark in the Morning Music*, the patient computer doc, actually made house calls.

Heidi Cusick for inspiration and votes of confidence.

Zida Borcich, and *Zida Borcich Letterpress*, for cover design and much more.

Anna Taylor of *Bookmakers*, for fine tuning and style.

HERBS *for* TERRIFIC TURKEY

INTENSELY ITALIAN HERBS

HERBES DE PROVENCE

CLOUDS' BLEND HERBS
Superb Seafoods, Salads, and Sauces

HERBS for BEAUTIFUL BEANS

HERBS for GLORIOUS GOULASHE

INTRODUCTION

In eighteen years of professional cooking, and some years before that in France, cooking for family and friends, I have used about every herb in the Western repertoire. In my restaurants and later my catering business, I realized that certain combinations were outstandingly versatile and useful, due to their natural affinity, and that these blends were always on the front of the stove. So I decided to make them available to other cooks, along with suggestions for their use. I think you will find them as indispensable as I do, and that you will discover your own new ways to use them.

This book is written for cooks at various levels of experience, to show how **Good Thyme Herb Blends** can be used in familiar everyday fare, and also, I hope, to give some new ideas. You will find a broad range of techniques, adapted for the home, but mostly you'll find robust, realistic food which defies fashion and uses readily available ingredients. My customers over the years have taught me how much people appreciate good food approached with common sense and a little style. Whether traditional or nouvelle, these are the real secret ingredients.

Bon Appetit!

Anise—One of the anise family, a small oval seed known for its licorice taste, slightly sweet. Native to the Middle East and Eastern Mediterranean, it was used in Europe by the 14th century and brought to the New World by early colonists. Anise is widely used as a digestive, and in India, to sweeten the breath.

Basil—Available in many exotic varieties, including cinnamon and lemon; important to Italians, French, and especially Californians. Large oval leaves are bright green, with a warm earthy smell suggesting clove. The essential oil is used in aromatherapy to allay mental fatigue.

Black Pepper—Once worth literally its weight in gold, now the most common spice in the Western world. Black peppercorns are the sun-dried and fermented unripe fruit of the vine Piper Nigrum.

Caraway—Member of the same aromatic family as parsley, but often confused with cumin. This hard brown oval seed is widely used in Jewish and central European cuisine to flavor breads, sausages, soups, sauerkraut, cabbage and cheeses.

Chilies—The capsicum family includes some 200 kinds of chilies and sweet peppers, originating in tropical America and spread worldwide. Ripe fresh chilies are dried and ground or crushed into flakes, adding savor and life to a wide variety of cuisines.

2

Cilantro—The delicate leaf of the coriander plant, cilantro's flavor is unlike that of the seed, and is essential in Mexican and Chinese dishes. The taste is so distinctive that it is often passionately loved or hated. Dried, it's much milder.

Coriander—A pale round or oval seed essential in curry powders, used for both savory and sweet dishes, and whose essential oil flavors chocolate. Now cultivated world wide, coriander's spread from the Middle East is documented back 3000 years, including its appearance in Massachusetts before 1670.

Cumin—Also essential to curry powders, this oval light-brown seed is a pungent and distinctive part of the cuisines of Mexico, North Africa, India, and the Middle East. Native to the Nile, it was spread to the New World by Spanish explorers.

Curry Powder—Indian cooks blend hundreds of curries, or masalas, but the basic ingredients are chilies, mustard seeds, fenugreek seeds, ground turmeric, fresh curry leaves, coriander, cumin, ginger, and sometimes cinnamon.

Dill Seed—Used in Medieval times for love and against witchcraft, dill is grown for both seed and weed. In northern European and Russian cuisine, the flat, oval seeds appear most commonly in pickles, breads, stews, potatoes and seafood. They are rich in mineral salts and beneficial for stomach and digestive ailments.

3

Fennel—Similar in taste to anise, cultivated since pre-Roman times for digestion and eyesight, scorpion and snake bites, and as protection against witchcraft. It is important in Italian, Iraqi, and Indian cuisine, and in Europe as a seasoning for fish.

Lavender—Often found in sachets for its lovely fragrance, but rarely in food. It is essential for accenting Herbes de Provence.

Lemon Peel—Dried and minced, it accents many dishes with a light citrus touch.

Marjoram—Used in the Middle Ages as a perfume, the mild green leaves impart their distinctive touch to Italian seasonings, Hungarian meat dishes, pizzas, eggs, and with fish such as haddock. Infused in teas, they soothe the nerves, help with sleep and relieve seasickness, among other miracles.

Oregano—Closely related to marjoram and used very similarly, it is an essential flavor in Italian and Mexican cuisine. Ancient Egyptians treasured it for its power to heal, disinfect, and preserve.

Paprika—A popular red chili powder, sweet or slightly pungent with a faint bitter aftertaste. It is esential to Hungarian and many Balkan dishes, as well as widely used in Spain.

Rose Petals—First cultivated in Persia and China, roses have lent their fragrance to scented waters, jellies, wines and candies for centuries. They are a versatile edible, and reputed to soothe skin, cleanse the blood and tone capillaries.

4

Sage—Known by the ancients to promote longevity, the gray-green downy leaf is a valuable aid in digesting fatty foods, both sweet and savory. Often used with poultry, it is also delicious with other meats and in sauces, or as an infusion for teas and vinegars.

Savory—Peppery and spicy, the Romans valued its disinfectant and aphrodisiac qualities. Bees love it, and its marriage with other herbs such as thyme is sublime.

Tarragon—Very important in French cuisine, the glossy, long, narrow leaves impart a warm, subtle, distinctive flavor, bittersweet and peppery at once. It is used with salads, vinegars, omelettes, herb butters, poultry and fish, also as a digestive.

Thyme—Most versatile of all, used in Roman soldiers' baths to increase vigor, by the Egyptians for embalming, and in the Middle Ages "to enable one to see the Fairies." It aids digestion of fats, enhances most meats and poultry, is essential to stocks, marinades, stuffings, soups and stews, and flavors Benedictine liqueur. If I had only one herb, it would be Thyme.

GLOSSARY

Most of the terms used in this book will be familiar. Here are a few which may not be:

Deglaze: to stir liquid (stock, water, or wine) into a hot pan in which ingredients have been sautéed or sweated. This dissolves stuck-on and carmelized residues and absorbs their flavors into the liquid, which is then used to complete the recipe.

Parboil: to briefly plunge ingredients, usually vegetables, into boiling water, then drain them, before preparing them further. This softens them and removes strong odors or tastes.

Reduce: to cook liquids or sauces over high heat to evaporate a great deal and thus concentrate the flavors.

Roux: the classic thickener made with roughly equal parts of flour and fat, usually butter. Flour is stirred into the melted fat, making a paste, then thinned by whisking in drippings, stock, wine, water, milk, or cream. It is simmered further to the right consistency.

Simmer: to cook slowly just at the point where a liquid forms lazy bubbles, but doesn't actually boil. Important in cooking meat, where a boil will toughen it.

Sweat: to cook juicy vegetables, especially onions, on low heat, covered and stirring occasionally, until they are soft, golden, or darker if you wish. This develops and concentrates their flavors.

Recipes using

HERBS for TERRIFIC TURKEY

**Thyme, Savory, Sage, Curry Powder,
Paprika, and Dried Red Chilies**

DEBRA DAWSON'S

HERBS   FOR

TERRIFIC
TURKEY
All Poultry & Game

HERBS FOR
TERRIFIC TURKEY

In the catering business, **turkey** is a standard for large and small groups. The problem is: How do you transform it into something wonderful? The solution is: with herbs!

I have always loved curry in all types of poultry, but curried turkey? Not exactly Thanksgiving fare, and hard to explain to relatives or customers. The *Terrific Turkey Blend* was created when I realized that a touch of curry in a still somewhat traditional blend could create a surprising twist. And it has proven more versatile than I ever imagined. So treat your guests to what my customers have so enjoyed—terrific turkey, poultry and game.

Terrific Turkey Ingredients

1 onion, quartered and stuck with two whole cloves
1 carrot, quartered
your turkey, stuffed or not, 12–18 pounds
2–3 tsp. salt
black pepper
3 Tbsp. *Terrific Turkey Herbs*
2 cups water or stock
1 cup Madeira or sherry

TERRIFIC TURKEY

For a different and delicious roast turkey:

Choose a roasting pan large enoungh to hold your bird comfortably. Sprinkle the pan and the *turkey* liberally with *salt, pepper*, and *Terrific Turkey Herbs*. If it's unstuffed, sprinkle the cavity as well. Put the *onion* and *carrot* beside the turkey to flavor the pan juices, then discard or nibble them later.

Roast it uncovered at 400° for 60 to 90 minutes, depending on size, until skin is browned and crisp. Then baste all at once with *water* or *stock* and *Madeira or sherry*. Reduce to 350°, cover and roast, basting occasionally with pan juices, until the meat juices run clear when a thigh is pierced with a fork. This should take only another 1–2 hours, again depending on size. And of course, be sure to roast it 30–45 minutes longer if it is stuffed.

Traditional recipes call for very long roasting times, but for a moister turkey, don't over-cook it! Allow 15 minutes resting time before carving; meanwhile strain the pan juices and use for sauce or gravy (see page 12).

Turkey is so easy and economical, why wait for the holidays? Unstuffed, it's simple as roasting a chicken, and even a small one can give a blessing of leftovers.

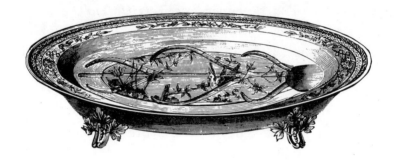

Wonderful Sauce Ingredients

the juice from roasting and basting the bird
1 more tsp. *Terrific Turkey Herbs*
2 Tbsp. cornstarch dissolved in ¼ cup cold water
2–3 Tbsp. Dijon-style mustard
tablespoon of honey (optional)
salt and pepper to taste

A WONDERFUL SAUCE
USING PAN JUICES

Your turkey can simply be served sliced in the warm juices, but if you want to go further, try this, and say goodbye forever to dried-out, lukewarm turkey.

Follow the preceding directions for roasting the bird, then remove it from the pan to cool for fifteen minutes before carving. Meanwhile, strain the *pan juices* into a saucepan; allow the fat to rise for a moment, then degrease by quickly blotting the surface with paper towels. You should have about 3 cups of juices.

Gently bring to a boil, add *Terrific Turkey Herbs*, and reduce for a few minutes for a slightly thicker sauce. Or, another way to thicken the juices further without the fat of a flour gravy is to add *cornstarch* dissolved in cold water, then stir and simmer gently for 5 minutes more while you carve the bird. Remove from the heat, stir in *mustard*, and if you like the idea, *a tablespoon of honey*. Add *salt and pepper* to taste. Pour the sauce into a deep preheated serving dish and keep it very hot, but not boiling. At the last minute, the sliced meat can be placed right in this dish.

The beauty of this technique is that you do not have to overcook the turkey, which so often is the ruin of the bird! Into the hot juices you can carefully place slices which are even slightly pink and they will cook through on the way to the table. Result: turkey which is moist, juicy and fragrant!

A SEA STORY

Sausage and sauerkraut stuffing for poultry is a French culinary tradition. The story behind *our* version of it is a bit long to tell in detail, but in brief, here goes:

It was Thanksgiving, 1975. Jacques Péré and I were co-owners of the *Café de la Grange* on Main Street in Mendocino, and also of a large old gaff-rigged schooner which we were trying desperately to bring up from the San Francisco Bay for repairs in Fort Bragg. Sailing out of Bodega Bay, we were caught at nightfall in a sudden, violent storm, and the boat began to disintegrate. With a broken main boom, clogged bilge pumps, a damaged rudder, and no radio, by Point Arena we were definitely sinking. Only an Alaskan fisherman knew we were at sea; he radioed for help, and the Coast Guard saved us in a dramatic air-sea rescue. Now we were stranded in Bodega Bay with the damaged boat and of course, *no car*.

It was now Wednesday, and meanwhile we had fifty reservations at our Café for Thanksgiving dinner on Thursday. A freezing rain was falling, and Jacques and I were hitchhiking up a deserted California Route One.

Darkness caught us at Point Arena, and if you've ever been to Point Arena, you'll know what that means. We huddled miserably in the Arena Café and decided it was not our week. The chances of someone driving from there to Mendocino in this weather were nil, minus something. It *definitely* wasn't our week.

But, wait, who should blow into the Café? A United Parcel driver! *Our* local UPS driver! Mendocino bound! We fell on him, but he refused: "No way, it's absolutely forbidden." Ensued a desperate discussion, and in the end, we were smuggled on board and off for home. What we said to that driver I never will tell . . .

Jacques had phoned his son to have the turkeys defrosted, and the plan was to rise at dawn, shop for the other ingredients, and serve dinner as if nothing . . . Well, imagine our dismay—everything was, naturally, closed! How we made dinner that day is yet another story, but the stuffing was born of what we had on hand: almonds, sausage, sauerkraut and rice. We borrowed cranberry sauce (yes, for fifty) from the Mendocino Hotel, our astonished but generous neighbor, and had a Thanksgiving dinner that couldn't be beat.

I never stuff a turkey without remembering that year.

Stuffing Ingredients

For a medium turkey, approximately 14 pounds:

1 cup almonds, oven-toasted till crunchy, 10–15 min.
1 onion, finely minced
2 Tbsp. butter, oil or margarine
¾ cup rice (white converted is safest, but your
    favorite brown or wild rice mix is great, too)
2 cups water or stock
½ tsp. salt
a 32-oz. jar of gourmet sauerkraut
4 garlic cloves, finely minced
1 apple, finely chopped
1 lb. ground pork sausage
    (or 4 eggs, if you don't eat pork)
½ tsp. pepper
2 Tbsp. *Terrific Turkey Herbs*
1 tsp. salt (or less, since sauerkraut is salty)
¼ cup sour cream

SAUSAGE and SAUERKRAUT STUFFING

Toast the *almonds* on a cookie sheet at 350° for 10–15 minutes. In a heavy saucepan, sauté *onion* until translucent in *butter, oil or margarine*. Add *rice* and sauté *rice* and *onion* together briefly, a minute at most, add *water or stock* (stock is best), and *salt*. Simmer, covered, no more than 15 minutes for white rice, 30 for brown, or until rice is still quite firm.

Meanwhile, drain *sauerkraut* and rinse it well or not, depending on how tangy you like your food. (I wouldn't rinse at all, but my husband wants it really washed, so we compromise.) Drain well. Mince *garlic* in the food processor, then *almonds*, until large chunks are gone, but not too fine. Now chop the *apple*. In a large bowl, combine everything, then test for seasoning by frying a bite and tasting it. Stuff the turkey fore and aft, and roast according to directions on page 9 for **Terrific Turkey**. Keep the stuffing warm while you carve, and serve with the hot pan juices.

Instead of drawing moisture from the bird as a bread stuffing would, this mixture will add liquid and will give a wonderful tang to the drippings. It's always fun to serve this surprising treat to guests who would never imagine such a combination. Enjoy!

CREAM OF
CARROT SOUP

What would we do without carrots? Available year round, colorful, inexpensive and healthy, we tend to take them for granted and to forget that the humble root can give some sophisticated results. For the seven years I made soup for the *Chocolate Moosse Café* on Kasten Street in Mendocino, carrots were the one ingredient (besides onions and garlic) that I could never be without. In everyday French cuisine, cream of carrot soup is a standard, upon which each chef sets his or her mark, but in America one sees it very seldom. It just doesn't occur to us. Here is a version which I love and often made for the *Chocolate Moosse Café*.

In a heavy-bottomed 6-quart stock pot, melt *butter or oil* (butter is best) over low heat. Add the onion, diced finely, and sweat, covered, over low heat until golden brown, stirring occasionally. I use the French term "to sweat" (*faire suer*) the onions instead of sauté, because they are deliberately stewed very slowly and not at all sautéed. This develops a wonderful flavor base for any soup or stew. Meanwhile, finely chop *one clove garlic* (not more, as too much garlic does not agree with this soup) with *jalapeño pepper or a few dried red chili flakes.*

Peel *carrots* (or scrub thoroughly) and remove ends. Slice them and add to the pot with garlic, potato, and jalapeño when the onions are golden and almost a paste. Add *bay leaf, salt* and *white pepper, Terrific Turkey Herbs, tomato paste and chicken stock,* or even better, veal stock. Try also with homemade stock from a turkey roasted with *Terrific Turkey Herbs*.

Simmer 20–30 minutes until the carrots are very soft. Drain them, keeping the liquid. Purée all or some of the carrots and return them to the pot with the stock. Add *milk, cream, and sherry*. Simmer a few more minutes and correct seasoning. If you want it saltier, add a little *soy sauce*. Garnish with fresh chopped *parsley* or *chives,* or a sprinkle of *paprika or nutmeg*.

Cream of Carrot Ingredients

3 Tbsp. butter or oil
2 medium onions
1 clove garlic
a half-inch piece of jalapeño pepper
4 lb. of carrots, about 12 medium
a large peeled potato, about one pound, diced
1 bay leaf
1 tsp. salt
¼ tsp. white pepper
1 tsp. *Terrific Turkey Herbs*
6 cups chicken stock, (or a 49-oz can)
2 Tbsp. tomato paste
soy sauce to taste
½ cup heavy cream and milk to desired consistency
¼ cup sherry

MARINADE for BARBECUED CHICKEN or TURKEY

A few hours before you are going to barbecue—or even the night before—place your chicken pieces in a deep dish with this fragrant marinade. For each chicken:

½ small onion, finely sliced
2 large garlic cloves, crushed with a knife handle
a half inch slice from a jalapeño pepper, coarsely chopped
    or ¼ tsp. hot pepper flakes
¼ cup rice vinegar
¼ cup dry white wine
1 Tbsp. *Terrific Turkey Herbs*
ground pepper to taste
1 Tbsp. soy sauce
½ cup cold-pressed peanut oil or olive oil
a few drops of strong sesame oil (optional)

Turn the pieces over in the marinade as often as you think of it, then remove and dry them to reduce flare-up on the grill. Sprinkle with more herbs, and continue brushing with the marinade again when the meat is half cooked. Look for clear juices when the meat is pricked with a fork, and turn often to prevent burning.

ROASTED GARLIC on the SIDE

In this time of lighter eating and lighter sauces, puréed vegetables and flavored oils often replace the butter and flour to dress up our plates and palates. Garlic, long known to keep the doctor away, is at the top of the flavor list. Roasted whole with *Terrific Turkey Herbs*, or roasted and puréed, it is lean, subtle, and versatile. Try this:

Preheat oven to 300°. Choose six heads of firm new garlic, and slice carefully across the top—not the root— of each, removing the outer skin and exposing the top of each inner clove. Tuck them snugly into a baking dish. Sprinkle with *one tablespoon Terrific Turkey Herbs*, and pour over them *1/4 cup of good extra virgin olive oil*. Bake them covered for one hour, or more if they aren't yet squishy-soft.

The garlic heads can be placed on a plate whole, to be squeezed out by each diner as a sweet, earthy condiment to any meat or poultry. The touch of curry in *Terrific Turkey Herbs* makes this a natural condiment for a curry supper. Or, purée the soft pulp with another dash of herbs, and mix it into *mashed potatoes*, or *puréed carrots, beans* or *legumes*. Mix the purée with *softened butter* for the best garlic bread ever. Add it to *mayonnaise* for a milder, richer aioli. These mixtures can be used to thicken other sauces, or as sauces themselves. If you've never eaten roasted garlic, you'll be amazed at its sweetness—it's quite unlike the assertive raw state!

Chicken with Lentils Ingredients

Serves four

1 cup lentils
1 large frying chicken
3 Tbsp. flour
1 small onion, finely diced
1 Tbsp. *Terrific Turkey Herbs*
½ tsp. black pepper
½ tsp. salt
2 Tbsp. peanut or olive oil
1 cup dry white wine
⅓ cup or ½ small can tomato paste
1 medium sized eggplant (skin can stay on)
1 bay leaf
1 tsp . salt and a sprinkle of pepper
1 Tbsp. *Terrific Turkey Herbs*
water or chicken stock to cover, 3–4 cups

SIMMERED CHICKEN
with LENTILS and EGGPLANT

I love *eggplant*—its dramatic good looks, its versatility and its assertive character. During the years of soups for the *Chocolate Moosse Café*, I'd have been lost without eggplant; it was a chameleon vegetable, ready to adapt to a hundred preparations. Making soup, I discovered the affinity of chicken, lentils, eggplant and curry. Try this:

Put *lentils* to soak in cold water for an hour or so. Quarter the *chicken* and dust with a mixture of *flour, Terrific Turkey Herbs, salt and pepper*. Brown gently on all sides in a heavy pot in *peanut* or *olive oil*. Remove chicken pieces, pour off most of the fat, and quickly sauté the *onion*. Add the *wine* and stir to deglaze. Whisk in *tomato paste* and add *eggplant,* diced neatly or split lengthwise and sliced finely across, depending on how you want it to look. Add drained *lentils, bay leaf, salt, pepper, and Terrific Turkey Herbs*. Add *water* or *chicken stock* to just cover and place chicken pieces neatly on top.

Bring to boil then *simmer* covered, *not boiling*, for about 45 minutes until lentils and eggplant are soft and chicken juices run clear when pricked. Make sure the liquid doesn't all evaporate or it will stick. Salt and pepper to taste, and serve with rice, plain yoghurt and chutneys. If you love curry add more of your favorite *curry powder*. This combination is also great with lamb instead of chicken, and just as easy to prepare.

23

TERRIFIC TOFU

Tofu, like turkey, has a reputation of being boring. But it doesn't have to be! Try it like this:

Cut each of the two blocks in a *1 pound package of tofu* horizontally into two steaks of one inch thick. Drain it well; pat dry.

Mix the following in a flat bowl:

2 tsp. Herbs For Terrific Turkey (preferably ground in a spice grinder), *2 Tbsp. flour, 1/2 tsp. salt*, and a few turns of *freshly ground pepper*.

Pat each tofu piece gently into the flour-herb mixture on each side, then sauté gently over medium heat in a heavy skillet with *1 Tbsp. butter* and *1 Tbsp. olive oil* until golden brown, about 4 minutes to a side. Squeeze *1 tsp. fresh lemon juice* on each piece, garnish with another *lemon slice* and *fresh parsley*, and serve with *sweet-hot mustard*.

As a variation, add a few drops of strong *sesame oil* to the sauté pan, or substitute cold-pressed peanut oil for the olive oil. Garnish with *sesame seeds* and *fresh cilantro*. With a steamed vegetable and rice this is a wonderfully light and satisfying meal. Even the meat eaters at my address approve! Serves four.

DELICIOUS!

APPLE, ONION, and POTATO TARTE

This is an adaptation of a Swiss dish with the unlikely name of **cholera**, which uses leeks instead of onions. Leeks are grand if you have them. Serves four.

Parboil *two whole medium potatoes*, skins on, for fifteen minutes, then drain and cool. Core and finely slice *two ripe apples* and *a large onion*; parboil them together for five minutes, then drain and cool. Meanwhile make a *pie crust* from your favorite recipe, or *puff paste*, or *filo dough*. If using filo, defrost by package directions, then lightly *butter* and stack at least eight sheets. Install the crust in a deep pie or quiche mold (tuck overhanging filo edges back in along the sides) and prebake ten minutes. (Lining the crust with foil keeps it erect during prebaking.) Slice the cooled *potatoes*, skins on or off, and layer half into the tarte. Layer on half the *apples* and *onions*, remaining potatoes, then apples and onions neatly on top. Dot with chunks of *sweet butter*.

Beat together *three large eggs, four ounces cream cheese, one half cup cream, 1 tsp. Terrific Turkey Herbs, 1 tsp. salt, and freshly ground pepper*. Pour over the tarte and bake forty-five minutes at 350°. A lower fat alternative is to use *ricotta* in place of cream cheese and *milk* for cream—or do as the Swiss do, using *Gruyère cheese*. It's lovely.

QUICK AND EASY EVERYDAY USES
for TERRIFIC TURKEY HERBS

Sprinkle liberally on any chicken or fish before broiling, with salt, pepper and a light brushing of olive oil.

Add to water when making white or brown rice, for a delicious curry accent.

Add to flour when dusting chicken pieces for fried chicken, for a new twist to an old favorite.

Add to stir-frying vegetables wherever a touch of curry would be welcome.

Add to your favorite vinaigrette for a new salad flavor.

A note for dieters: My friend Gitta Pierrot uses **Terrific Turkey Herbs** on baked potatoes, and swears that she needs no butter that way. She's right!

Grind **Terrific Turkey Herbs** in a spice grinder and toss with popcorn, too.

Recipes using

INTENSELY ITALIAN HERBS

Oregano, Thyme, Fennel Seed, Basil, Marjoram,
Paprika, and Dried Red Chilies

DEBRA DAWSON'S

HERBS   FOR

INTENSELY
ITALIAN

Tomato Sauces, Pasta & Pizza

INTENSELY ITALIAN HERBS

When the *Chocolate Moosse Café* opened in 1981 in Mendocino, they had only a soup warmer and a toaster oven, so I began supplying their soups and entrees from my shop. We decided to feature lasagne as a hearty lunch entrée for those foggy coastal days, and it quickly became a mainstay of their menu. For the sauce, I needed a ready blend of Italian-style seasonings with real gusto, so I developed the *Intensely Italian Blend*. With whole fennel seeds, oregano, basil and marjoram, it contains all the herbs needed for the perfect tomato-based sauce.

Almost everyone makes pasta, from the family version of everyday spaghetti to sophisticated preparations of homemade raviolis or cannellonis. A well-made sauce is often the secret which lifts the everyday to the sublime. Use *Intensely Italian Herbs* to create fine sauces, soups, and in many other ways—wherever an Italian accent is needed.

Lasagne Sauce Ingredients

Makes a gallon

2 large onions, finely chopped
½ cup olive oil
8 garlic cloves
half a jalapeño pepper
2 lb. ground pork or Italian sausage
    (chicken or turkey sausage is fine, too)
½ cup *Intensely Italian Herbs*
two 28-oz. cans ground tomatoes
½ cup tomato paste
2 tsp. salt
¼ tsp. pepper

The FAMOUS LASAGNE of the
Chocolate Moosse Café, Mendocino, California

In a large, heavy-bottomed saucepan, sweat *onions* gently in *olive oil,* covered and stirring frequently until they are golden brown and very reduced *but not too darkened or blackened in any way.* This could take a good half hour. When they are a golden brown paste, add *garlic* and *jalapeño pepper,* minced together very fine in processor.

Add *sausage* and stir vigorously to break into fine bits and sauté slightly. (You can use ground beef or turkey but not more than half or it won't be as good.) Add *Intensely Italian Herbs* and *ground tomatoes.* If you have some good fresh tomatoes, chop them and add as well. Julia Child uses canned ground tomatoes and so should we all, as good fresh ripe ones are so hard to come by in most seasons. Fill one of the cans two thirds full of *water* and whisk in *tomato paste, salt,* and *pepper.* Add this to the sauce.

Simmer at least 30 minutes, stirring often to prevent sticking. This will make a good gallon of sauce, which is far too much for a single lasagne, so freeze half of it for another day, or better yet, make 2 or 3 lasagne while you're at it and freeze them fully assembled.

This sauce can be made meatless for a *vegetarian lasagne.* Just add your favorite vegetables.

For Lasagne Assembly:

Serves eight

1 lb. good lasagne noodles
½ lb. grated mozzarella
½ lb. grated sharp white cheddar
1 cup grated parmesan
1 pint cottage cheese or ricotta

Cook *lasagne noodles* according to package directions. Do *not* overcook. Drain and rinse with cold water and put back into the pot in cold water while you work. This keeps the noodles separated, and also rinses your fingers each time you grab some noodles.

Cover the bottom of a 9 × 11 baking pan with sauce, then build the layers with noodles, more sauce, and the cheeses: *mozzarella* and *sharp white cheddar*, mixed; *parmesan*, and *cottage cheese*. *Ricotta* is great too, and traditional, but I like cottage cheese and it's much easier to work with. Finish top with sauce and mozzarella blend; parmesan on the top will blacken and dry out. Bake at 350° for fifty minutes and dive in. **Delicious**!

Lasagne can be made in many varieties, with or without meat, so don't hesitate to improvise. Keep reading for some ideas to escape from the tomato and cheese theme.

LOTS of LASAGNE

Make a *Balsamella*, or white sauce: Melt *1/2 stick sweet butter*, stir in *1/4 cup unbleached flour* until smooth; let stand for ten minutes to eliminate raw flour taste, then gradually add *2 cups hot milk*, whisking constantly over low heat until thick and creamy. Cool and use like this:

1. Sweat *2 cleaned and sliced leeks* in *2 Tbsp. butter or oil*, with *one finely diced carrot, 4 sliced mushrooms*, and *1 clove minced garlic*. Add *1 cup rinsed lentils, 1 Tbsp. Intensely Italian Herbs*, and *1 cup chopped tomatoes, fresh* or *canned*. Simmer 30 minutes, barely covered with water. Salt and pepper to taste, and use as you would tomato sauce, previous pages. Topped with *balsamella*, this can be cheeseless, or you can layer with your favorite *cheeses*.

2. Pour some *balsamella* into the bottom of a pan, then a layer of cooked *noodles*, a thin, even layer of *salmon fillet*, more noodles, a layer of fresh *spinach*, steamed, chopped, and squeezed dry, a teaspoon of *Intensely Italian Herbs*, another layer of *pasta*, and more *balsamella*. Top with grated *Romano* or *Asiago cheese*. Very delicate and fine.

3. Lasagne with *capers and eggplant* is a Sicilian classic. The eggplant can be fried or baked in thin slices, layered with *fresh pasta* or boiled *lasagne noodles*, *balsamella*, and a simple *tomato sauce* with *capers*. It is topped with *bread crumbs* and *balsamella*. Yum.

Creamy Lasagne Ingredients

    1   medium onion
    3   Tbsp. butter or olive oil
    2   garlic cloves
    2   Tbsp. *Intensely Italian Herbs*
    a hefty dash of cayenne pepper
    ½   tsp. salt
    black pepper
    4   level Tbsp. flour
    3   cups half and half , warmed
    2   Tbsp. Dijon-style mustard
    hot salted water
    1   lb. spinach lasagne noodles
    1   cup ricotta cheese
    another 1 Tbsp. mustard
    1   cup grated sharp white cheddar cheese
    1   cup grated Asiago cheese

CREAMY LASAGNE, HOT and CHEESY

Make the sauce: Sweat very finely-chopped *onion* in *butter or olive oil* over low heat and covered. When pale golden add *garlic, Intensely Italian Herbs, cayenne pepper, salt,* freshly-ground *black pepper* and *flour.* Stir to make a roux, then slowly whisk in *half and half.* Stir over low heat until smooth, thick, and creamy. Add *mustard.* Set aside and keep warm. Meanwhile boil water to cook *spinach lasagne noodles* according to directions, being careful not to overcook. Drain and place in cold water. Mix *ricotta cheese* with *1 Tbsp. mustard* and another *pinch of cayenne.*

Assemble by coating the bottom of an 8 × 14 or 10 × 10 or equivalent baking dish with a thin layer of sauce. Cover with a layer of *noodles* lengthwise, more sauce, *grated white sharp cheddar cheese,* more noodles lengthwise and finally the remaining *cream sauce.* Top with *grated Asiago cheese.* Bake at 350° for 35–40 minutes.

Serve as a hearty vegetarian main course or a sumptuous side dish to a lean entrée.

PIZZA with PIZAZZ

Extra lasagne sauce is great on spaghetti or pizza. Cover your homemade or premade pizza dough with (for a medium pizza) *2 cups lasagne sauce* (page 30) mixed with an additional *1/4 cup tomato paste*. Sprinkle with *1 Tbsp. Intensely Italian Herbs* and add any of the following or your favorite toppings:

Sliced pepperoni or *linguisa* or *garlic sausage, mushrooms, diced ham, roasted green or red peppers, ground beef* or *turkey, sun-dried tomatoes, olives, anchovies,* or *capers.* Top with *grated mozzarella, parmesan* and *romano.* Bake at 400° for 20 minutes or according to pizza dough directions.

SPAGHETTI with
INTENSELY ITALIAN HERBS

Make spaghetti sauce according to directions for lasagne sauce (page 31), using half *ground premium beef* and half *ground pork*, or all *ground beef*, or *ground turkey*, as you like. For vegetarian sauce, add *sliced mushrooms, zucchini or summer squash*, or *fresh peas*. Add some chopped fresh basil at the end of simmering, and toss with spaghetti or flat fettucine. Finish with your favorite cheese.

NEW CLASSIC MEAT LOAF
with OLIVES and MUSTARD

2 lb. ground beef **or**
     1 lb. ground beef and l lb. ground veal or turkey
a small onion, finely chopped
2 garlic cloves, minced
2 Tbsp. Dijon-style mustard
2 Tbsp. *Intensely Italian Herbs*
a 4-oz. can chopped olives
2 tsp. soy sauce
ground pepper and a splash of Worcestershire
1 egg or ¼ cup cream cheese
¼ cup oat bran
2 Tbsp. wheat germ
a handful of chopped parsley

Meat loaf has been around for a long time and for good reason—it's quick, nourishing, comforting, and quite foolproof. Simply combine the ingredients and pat into a loaf pan or into a mound in an oven dish. If your meats are very lean, add another *egg* or it might be crumbly. Gently press **2 bay leaves** into the surface and bake for 1 hour at 350°, or microwave 17–20 minutes. You might even make two and freeze one.

Serve with a selection of mustards and horseradishes, a baked potato and little cornichon pickles.

Tomato Mushroom Soup Ingredients

For about a gallon:

2 Tbsp. butter
1 Tbsp. olive oil
2 medium onions
2 garlic cloves
¼ tsp. hot pepper flakes or a minced piece of jalapeño
a 14-oz can crushed tomatoes,
    or a pound of fresh ones plus 2 Tbsp. tomato paste
2 pounds mushrooms, diced or sliced
1 Tbsp. *Intensely Italian Herbs*
a 49-oz. can chicken stock or 6 cups homemade
1 Tbsp. Worcestershire
2 Tbsp. brown sugar
¼ cup barley
½ cup of your favorite small pasta shape
½ tsp. salt or to your taste, and pepper likewise
½ to one cup cream or milk

TOMATO MUSHROOM SOUP
with BARLEY

This soup was a favorite at the *Chocolate Moosse Café*. It's hard for me to make a small pot of soup (it freezes, and reheats another day), so if this recipe for a gallon is too much for you, just make half. Or make it all and invite some friends!

In a heavy-bottomed 6-qt. pot, melt *butter* and *olive oil* and add *onions*, finely chopped. Sweat covered over low heat, stirring to prevent sticking, until limp and golden browned. It is important to cook the onions down fully before adding the rest. Mince *garlic* and add to the pot with the *mushrooms* and cook 5 minutes to soften them. Add *tomatoes, Intensely Italian Herbs, Worcestershire, sugar*, and *chicken stock*.

When the soup has come to a boil, add the *barley* and simmer about 30 minutes until it is soft. Add the pasta for the last 15 minutes, and stir to prevent sticking. Add *salt and pepper* to taste and *cream*. (Leave out the cream on any part you might freeze.) Garnish with *fresh chopped parsley* or with *snips of fresh basil*, and serve with fresh **Herb Bread** (page 143).

39

FINOCCHIO AL FORNO
Three Ways with Fennel

Fennel bulb is very popular in Italy and France, and increasingly seen in American markets. It is eaten raw in salads, or cooked in various ways. Some ideas:

Use *one medium bulb* per person. Prepare by removing stems, the core at the bottom, and any stringy or discolored outer layer. Cut in half, and quarter or slice the halves. Soak in cold water for 30 minutes; then parboil in boiling salted water for about 10 minutes. Drain, and then:

1. Arrange in a buttered baking dish with bits of sautéed *sweet Italian sausage, 1 tsp. Intensely Italian Herbs, salt and pepper* to taste. Cover with *breadcrumbs, chunks of sweet butter,* and *1/4 cup grated parmesan.*

2. In France the sausage would likely be replaced by thin slivers of *ham,* and cheese of choice would be *Gruyère* or *Emmentaler,* with some Balsamella (page 33).

3. For each bulb, finely chop together *one anchovy fillet* and *one Tbsp. drained capers* with *one Tbsp. olive oil.* Toss with thin *fennel slices and 1 tsp. Intensely Italian Herbs.* Layer in a heavily olive-oiled baking dish, and moisten with *chicken stock.*

Bake all the above about 25 minutes at 350°.

MUSTARD HONEY
BALSAMIC VINAIGRETTE

1 garlic clove, finely minced
3 Tbsp. of your favorite mustard
3 Tbsp. honey
1 Tbsp. *Intensely Italian Herbs*
freshly ground black pepper
¼ cup balsamic vinegar
½ cup rice vinegar, or other fine vinegar
2 cups olive oil
    (or 1 cup olive and 1 cup walnut or grapeseed oil)

Mince *garlic* in food processor or by hand and add *mustard, honey, herbs and pepper*. Process or whisk together with the *vinegar*, gradually adding the *oil* and whisking or processing until emulsified and creamy. Toss with romaine, feta cheese, olives, roasted peppers, tomatoes and red onions, and garnish with chopped walnuts or pine nuts. Or use to dress pasta salads of all kinds. Store in a glass jar and use as needed.

POLENTA alla Fabia

My Swiss husband Arrigo has challenged me since I have known him to reproduce the polenta he remembers from his childhood. The way he tells it, his Italian mother stood by the stove for hours and stirred the fragrant yellow corn meal mush in its water bath, then when it was just right, turned it out  onto a wooden board where it would hold its shape of a round cake. It would then be cut into wedges with a thread slipped under and pulled up. The next day, it was fried in butter and served in a bowl with cold milk, or broiled with (what else?) Swiss cheese. We have done all this over the years and it's as delicious as he remembers. Or almost—is anything ever as delicious as we remember?

If the standing and stirring part sounds forbidding, don't give up on Polenta—it can be done in the oven with no fuss at all. Combine *4 cups of water* to *one of polenta*, a little *butter* and 1 tsp. *salt*, perhaps some *parmesan*, and bake in a buttered pan one hour at 350˚. These directions are on some sacks of polenta. For what to do next I am indebted to my husband's sister Fabia. She visited us and taught me some family secrets, including the fact that their mother hated to cook, and it was Dad who stirred the polenta. When *your* polenta is firmly set in the oven (about 45 minutes into the hour) cover the top with one of the following:

Four large onions thinly sliced and browned slowly until very brown but not black, in *two Tbsp. butter* and *two Tbsp. olive oil*, with *1 tsp. Intensely Italian Herbs* (my new family secret). Or:

A layer of your homemade *tomato sauce* (page 30) with or without sausage. If available, cover the tomato sauce with a layer of sliced *fresh tomatoes*, then another sprinkle of *Intensely Italian Herbs*. Cover with grated *Gruyère* and broil until bubbly brown on top. At the hotel of some friends in Switzerland I once prepared this for a party by making a polenta sandwich with a layer of tomatoes and sauce in the middle *and* on top. An American in the kitchen.

If you want a polenta cake to cut into smaller shapes for broiling, do it stovetop in a heavy pot, with the same ingredients. Add polenta in a steady stream to boiling water, stir constantly til thick and smooth, then simmer, stirring often, for 30 minutes. Pour into a shallow buttered pan and allow to cool and set, then cut into any shape you fancy. It can now be broiled or fried.

Polenta is such a marvelous medium that I'm amazed it has only recently become fashionable. Try stirring one Tbsp. of *Intensely Italian Herbs* into the original water and cornmeal mix, then bake it plain, gently herbed. Or top it with *mushrooms, roasted green and red peppers, crumbled feta cheese,* or embed an *anchovy, an olive,* or some *capers* into individually shaped portions. Polenta is infinite!

Fish for the Grill Ingredients

Serves four

2 lb. firm-fleshed white fish

Marinade:
  a juicy lemon
  ¼ cup dry white wine
  2 Tbsp. olive oil
  1 garlic clove
  several slices red onion
  1 Tbsp. *Intensely Italian Herbs*
  ½ tsp. paprika

Sauce:
  the marinade plus:
    ½ tsp. salt
    fresh ground pepper
    ½ cube unsalted butter
    2 Tbsp. capers
    fresh chopped parsley

FISH for the GRILL
with HERBS and PAPRIKA

Choose thick fillets, at least 1 inch, of *very fresh fish*. Combine marinade ingredients. Turn the fillets in the marinade to coat them, then refrigerate together in a bowl for about 2 hours, turning occasionally. Remove fish from marinade and place in fish grilling basket or on an oiled, fine-meshed grill. Barbecue on an even, moderate fire, about 8 minutes per inch of thickness. Meanwhile, strain the marinade and heat it gently, adding *salt* and *fresh ground pepper*. Whisk in *unsalted butter* in several chunks; add *capers*. Place fish fillets in warmed serving dish and pour sauce over them.

Garnish with *chopped parsley* and serve with *new potatoes* and barbecued *zucchini*: halve the zucchini lengthwise, brush with *olive oil* and sprinkle lightly with *Intensely Italian Herbs*. Grill slowly until soft.

This method can also be used with great results for *chicken breast, turkey breast slices*, or even *pork chops or cutlets*.

Sprinkle any one of the versatile **Good Thyme Herb Blends** on meats or poultry before grilling or barbecuing for the wonderful flavor and aroma of toasted herbs. It's a simple pleasure well known to outdoor persons and lovers of barbecue. Try them all!

Eggplant Ingredients

1 eggplant
2–3 garlic cloves
½ cup pine nuts (or other nuts)
½ lb. ground veal
1 tsp. salt
1 tsp. white pepper
1 Tbsp. *Intensely Italian Herbs*
2 Tbsp. capers with 1 tsp. of their vinegar
3–4 ripe tomatoes or one 12-oz. can ground tomatoes
another tsp. *Intensely Italian Herbs*
½ cup parmesan or romano
3–4 Tbsp. olive oil
chopped pine nuts for garnish

By binding the stuffing with **4 eggs** and adding **1/2 cup of crumbled feta**, this is a fine vegetarian supper, hearty, tasty and unusual. You will want to salt carefully if using feta, as it is already so salty.

EGGPLANT STUFFED
with GROUND VEAL and CAPERS

I use eggplant with all six **Herb Blends**, mostly because I love it so much. Stuffed, one good-sized eggplant is a hearty meal for at least four persons. Try this; it's surprisingly quick and easy.

Halve an *eggplant* lengthwise and scoop out the pulp, leaving walls at least three-quarters of an inch thick. In a food processor, finely process *garlic* with *1/2 cup raw pine nuts*. Add *eggplant pulp* and process to fine dice. Turn into a bowl and stir in *salt, ground veal* (or *ground turkey* if you prefer), *white pepper, Intensely Italian Herbs*, and *capers*. Cut a little, fine slice off the bottom of each eggplant half so it will sit on a flat surface. Fill the halves, mounding as necessary.

Cover the bottom of a 2-inch-deep baking dish with *slices of fresh tomatoes* or canned ground tomatoes. Place eggplant halves on tomatoes and sprinkle with a little more *salt and pepper* and one more teaspoon of *herbs*. Place a slice of tomato on each eggplant half and sprinkle with *parmesan* or *romano*. Drizzle with *olive oil*. Bake one hour in a preheated 350° oven. Baste with a little *water* or *dry white wine* to prevent sticking or drying out of stuffing.

When done, slice carefully and arrange slices with stuffing on a heated serving platter. Pour on pan juices and garnish with *chives* and *chopped pine nuts*. *Rice* or *buttered noodles* is a perfect complement.

RISOTTO with PORCINI MUSHROOMS

With the first October rains on the Pacific Coast, I go slightly mad, abandon everything, and go mushroom hunting. The *boletus edulis*, or porcini, is abundant for a brief exhilarating time, and I gather for a whole year. Dried or fresh, they add incomparable flavor and richness to sauces, soups, or grains, as in this classic Italian dish.

Soak *one ounce dried porcini mushrooms* in *one cup dry white wine* for an hour at least. If you have fresh ones, finely slice about a pound. Slowly brown *a large red onion, diced*, in *4 Tbsp. olive oil* and *2 Tbsp. butter*, until limp and golden brown. If mushrooms are fresh, increase the heat and add them to the onions, tossing to sauté rather than stew. If dried, chop them coarsely, reserving the wine from soaking, and add to the skillet. Add *2 cloves garlic*, finely chopped with a handful of *Italian parsley*.

Add *2 cups raw rice*, Italian Arborio is best, and sauté all together, stirring for 5 minutes. Add *2 Tbsp. Intensely Italian Herbs*, the reserved *wine* and begin adding warmed *chicken stock*, stirring frequently, adding more only as it is absorbed by the rice. This will take 3–4 cups of stock, and about 25 minutes. When soft, add *1/2 cup parmesan, a big pinch of saffron, salt* and *freshly ground pepper* to taste, and serve immediately. It's a meal in itself or a sumptuous side dish. Serves six.

POULET PROVENÇALE
Roast Chicken with Fresh Tomatoes and Garlic

This dish was featured at a wedding supper at the Mendocino Woodlands. I thank my stepmother, Betty Barber, who finally convinced me to flour the chicken before baking it, which I had never done before tasting her wonderful barbecued chicken. Here's how we did it:

Use **4 breasts** or quarter a **large fryer.** Lightly coat each piece with the following mix, either by shaking in a paper bag or patting it into a large plate: **1/4 cup flour, 2 Tbsp. Intensely Italian Herbs, 1 tsp. salt,** and **1/2 tsp. pepper.** Roast in an oven dish at 400° for 30 minutes for thighs, 20 for breasts, until browned and sizzling. Meanwhile finely chop or press **2 large cloves garlic** and mix with **4 chopped ripe tomatoes.**

Remove chicken pieces briefly from the dish, pour off fat, and place the chopped tomatoes in the bottom. Replace chicken and add **3/4 cup water, stock,** or **dry white wine.** Bake 30 minutes more at 350°. Garnish with scissored snips of **fresh basil.** Serve with **polenta, fresh fettucine, white beans** or **risotto.**

Serves four.

49

QUICK AND EASY
with INTENSELY ITALIAN HERBS

The ultimate quick supper is *pasta*, so I recommend keeping a drawer full of all the sizes and shapes you can find. Always cook in lots of *boiling salted water* until *al dente*, still firm. Since pasta cools rapidly, place your serving dish in the sink, drain pasta over it, put the pasta back into the warm pot to be sauced or oiled, then finally, back into the drained (and now hot) serving dish. Off to the table, nice and warm. Here are some variations, quick and easy, for one pound pasta, to serve six as a main course.

Toss coquilles, torsades, or fettucine with a heated mix of *1/4 cup cognac, 1/2 cup cream* and *1 tsp. Intensely Italian Herbs*.

Parboil *one bunch of cleaned and cut broccoli* in lots of salted water for six minutes. Drain and keep this water to cook your *pasta*. Chop *10 anchovies* with *1/3 to 1/2 cup olive oil, 1 Tbsp. Intensely Italian Herbs*, and *more red pepper flakes*. Mix everything.

Make a *pasta salade* with *greek olives, lemon juice, slices of sautéed swordfish, garlic, olive oil, white wine, parsley*, and *Intensely Italian Herbs*.

Toss fine *spaghettini* with any *fresh vegetables*. Cut finely, they can steam over boiling pasta with a sprinkle of *Intensely Italian Herbs*. Very compact.

Recipes using

HERBES DE PROVENCE

Thyme, Savory, Anis Seed, Fennel Seed, Basil, and Lavender

D E B R A   D A W S O N'S

HERBES ᴰᴱ
PROVENCE
for Soups, Stews, Marinades

Menu du Dimanche
(Sunday in the Country)

Potage Germiny
Assiette de Crudities

Raie au Beurre Noir

Gigot d' Agneau a'la Ficelle
les Flageollets au Beurre
Salade de pis-en-lit

Fromages

Buisson de Meringues a'la Chantilly

HERBES DE PROVENCE

Herbes de Provence, an ancient combination, is my favorite herb blend. Just smelling it takes me back to the dry high plateaux of south-central France. A touch of lavender makes it truly unique.

Herbes de Provence are wonderful on any roasted or stewed meats, but their marriage with lamb in all its forms is particularly irresistible. During the late 1970s, when Jacques Péré and I operated the *Little River Café* on the Mendocino Coast, *Roast Leg of Lamb with Herbes de Provence* was our specialty.

Jacques re-created in the oven the delight of the timeless *Gigot à la Ficelle*, which we often made for Sunday visitors to our farm in France: A leg of lamb would be stuck with garlic, covered with salt, pepper and *Herbes de Provence*, and hung with a very heavy string in front of a robust fire in an open hearth. A large bowl collected the drippings and a basting of butter and water, which would be re-used to baste frequently. The basting liquid would be applied to the string itself before it attached to the leg of lamb. Wetted and re-dried by the fire, the string caused the meat to turn slowly and thus roast perfectly on all sides.

Our large walk-in fireplaces with oak mantles and floor-level hearths were perfect for this treatment, and I will never forget the thrill of the results.

LEG of LAMB
with HERBES DE PROVENCE

With my thanks to Jacques Péré, here is how to do it in your oven. Another thanks is in order, to my sister-in-law Fabia, who—being Swiss—takes it a step further. She wouldn't roast the leg of lamb without first marinating it for a day in the following mixture: *2 large cloves crushed garlic, 1/2 cup dry red wine, 1/2 cup olive oil, 1 Tbsp. Herbes de Provence, 4 black peppercorns, 1 clove* and *1/2 onion*, in chunks. Keep it in the refrigerator overnight, turning every few hours, except when you are sleeping.

Before marinating, have the butcher remove the little piece of bone at the shank end, or do it yourself with a sharp boning knife. Roast this in the pan for your dog.

To roast, remove fat in the thickest spots, leaving a little membrane of it all around to insure juiciness. Lard the leg with *little slivers of garlic*, especially around the bone. About *4 medium cloves* cut into several slivers each should do it, or more if you only want to taste a little lamb with your garlic.

Sprinkle the bottom of an oven dish with *salt*, and half the *Herbes de Provence*. Lay the roast with the fattest side up, then sprinkle again liberally with *salt* and *pepper*, and the rest of the *Herbes de Provence*. Roast in a preheated 450° oven until crusty brown and sizzling, about 45 minutes.

Only then, baste with water or **Madeira** or **port**, and replace in the oven for another 10 minutes (for 4 lb.) to 20 minutes (for 6 lb.)—this time at 350°.

Rest the leg of lamb for 10 minutes before carving. Depending on the size, it should still be quite rare in the center.

While you wait for the lamb to cool enough to carve, you can strain and reduce the juices a little, whisking in the optional *sweet butter*. As with the turkey (page 11), the beauty of this technique is that you can keep the copious pan juices piping hot—*not boiling*—then place into them the tender pink slices, just at serving. The center slices can arrive at the table *very* rare, and the outside ones less so, but moist and juicy! This gives you marvelous control of the doneness, which to me is the essence of good lamb.

Leg Of Lamb Ingredients

a leg of lamb, 4–6 lb.
4 medium cloves garlic
salt and pepper
3 Tbsp. **Herbes de Provence**
2 cups water or stock or
1 cup port or Madeira
    and 1 cup water or stock
a few chunks of sweet butter (optional)

White Beans Ingredients

1 lb. Great Northern or baby lima beans (2 cups)
1 small onion, stuck with 2 whole cloves
2 garlic cloves, minced
1 large carrot
½ tsp. salt
¼ tsp. black pepper
1 Tbsp. tomato paste
1 Tbsp. *Herbes De Provence*
2 Tbsp. butter
parsley
a chopped fresh tomato (optional), diced to 1-inch cubes
   Add your lamb bone if you've removed it.

WHITE BEANS with GARLIC
and HERBES DE PROVENCE

Also from the *Little River Café* repertoire, the absolutely best and most traditional side dish for the lamb:

Soak *beans* overnight in cold water. In France the bean of choice for serving with leg of lamb is the Flageollet, which is pale green and smaller than the lima, but they aren't easy to find here, so use the white ones and they'll be great. Drain and place in a 4 qt. saucepan with *onion,* quartered and stuck with *cloves, garlic, carrot,* peeled and sliced thin; *salt, black pepper* and *tomato paste.* Cover—plus about 2 inches—with *cold water* and bring to a boil.

Reduce heat to simmer and remove any scum which rises. When scum stops appearing (after about 5 minutes of skimming) add *Herbes de Provence,* cover and simmer 45–50 minutes until beans are tender. Check to be sure water is not all boiled off. Five minutes before serving, add chopped fresh tomato if you like the idea. Toss with *butter* and freshly chopped *parsley,* and serve with the slices of leg of lamb and their juices. I like the color and taste of simple *sliced carrots* as the second vegetable in this meal—pure and traditional.

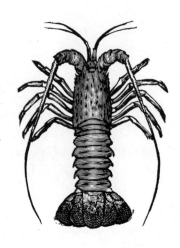

Fish Soup Ingredients

1 lb. cod or snapper fillets, and any shellfish you fancy
2 large onions, chopped or finely sliced
¼ cup olive oil
a 28-oz. can ground tomatoes
4 garlic cloves
½" piece jalapeño pepper or ½ tsp. red pepper flakes
1 Tbsp. *Herbes de Provence*
a bay leaf
2 chopped fresh tomatoes
2 qts. fish stock or clam juice, or half chicken broth
salt and pepper
3–4 large potatoes (optional), diced into 1-inch cubes
pinch of saffron

MEDITERRANEAN FISH SOUP, BOUILLABAISSE-STYLE

Another *Little River Café* specialty was our robust garlicky fish soup, made with *Herbes de Provence,* and our local red snapper or ling cod. Again I thank Jacques Péré for his easy version of the classic.

In a heavy-bottomed 4-qt. saucepan, sweat *onions* with *olive oil* over medium-low heat until limp and golden brown. Add *ground tomatoes, garlic* finely minced with *jalapeño pepper* (or *red pepper flakes*), *Herbes de Provence, bay leaf,* and *fresh tomatoes,* chopped. Cover with *stock* or *clam juice* (best is home-made stock from white fish heads and bones, but if this isn't possible, use canned clam juice). Bring it to boil and simmer for half an hour to set flavors, then *salt* and *pepper* to taste.

If you want this soup to be a hearty main dish chowder, add diced parboiled *potatoes* to the stock when it reaches a boil, then let them cook in the soup. (Stir or they'll stick.) Cut *cod* or *snapper fillets* into one-inch chunks and add, together with any *scallops,* only five minutes before serving, turning off the fire. The heat of the soup will cook them through. *Clams or mussels* can be added for the last minutes of cooking to steam open, or steamed separately and added last. Add *saffron* and a pinch more of *Herbes de Provence.*

Serve with **Herb Bread** (page 143), salad, and—very important—with *rouille* (next page).

59

I recently found a fascinating reference to bouillabaisse in an old book, *Le Folklore de la Provence*, by Claude Seignolle. He traces the origin of the word to Occitan, the old language of the southwest of France. *Lou boui abaisso* was a bouillon of fish, highly spiced, cooked on a high fire and rapidly, from whence the origin of the word: *Dou tems que boui abaisso*. (When it boils, pour it.) The bouillon was served on slices of bread, with the boiled fish on the side, accompanied by red peppers and garlic cloves, crushed in a mortar with boiled potatoes. Consider this an option for serving!

The fish soup (with fish *in* the soup) is served with a *rouille*—a tomato- and saffron-laced version of the traditional aioli. Here's how to do it:

**Rouille For Serving
with Bouillabaisse**

To *1 egg yolk* in a bowl, add *2 Tbsp. Dijon-style mustard*. Whisk gently with a *pinch of salt*. Begin to add *olive oil* in a very small trickle, whisking gently to "set" the mixture. Slowly add *olive oil*, only as the mixture will absorb, as you whisk. If it curdles, add *1 tsp. of mustard* to edge of mixture and gently incorporate to make the mayonnaise bind. Add *a few drops of vinegar* if it is too stiff. When you have about a cup, add *4 to 8 cloves garlic*, mortared or passed through a press, (you decide how much garlic you like) plus *2 Tbsp. tomato paste* and *a good pinch of saffron*. *Salt* a little to taste and add *a pinch of cayenne*. This will make a dollop for about 8 bowls of soup.

PORK ROAST PROVENÇALE

At a recent tasting of dishes made with herbs, mustard and honey, this delicious roast was a favorite. Remember that for tenderness and accurate timing, meats should be at room temperature before roasting.

Choose a lean pork roast, leg or loin is best, and if using a loin, remove the chine bone for easy carving between chops. Lard with *2–4 cloves garlic,* sliced to make several pieces. (Poke little slits with a small sharp knife and insert the garlic pieces.) Mix together *2 Tbsp. honey, 2 Tbsp. Dijon-style mustard,* and *1 Tbsp. Herbes de Provence.* Apply liberally to the *pork roast* before setting it fat side up into an oven dish sprinkled with *salt* and *pepper. Salt* and *pepper* top of roast, and sprinkle with another *1 tsp. Herbes de Provence.*

Roast at 350° for 25 minutes per pound. When it's brown, in about one hour, pour off fat then begin basting with *1/2 cup dry sherry* and *1/2 cup water.* When it's finished (internal temperature 160°), remove the roast to a heated platter, allow to rest 15 minutes, then slice it and use the pan juices for sauce or gravy. Some *new potatoes* can be roasting with the meat for the last 45 minutes, and *carrots* as well. With a salad, it's easy, complete and tasty.

Stuffing for Honey Mustard Chicken

For one large chicken or three Cornish game hens:

½ oz. dried wild mushrooms:
 Porcini or chanterelles are wonderful. Soak them
 overnight in champagne, wine or brandy,
 drain and chop. Put the liquid back in the stuffing.
half a small onion, chopped and sautéed in butter
½ cup raisins soaked in ¼ cup brandy or port
1 cup wild rice—prepare as directed, but drain
 ten minutes before fully cooked
1 tsp. *Herbes de Provence*
1 garlic clove, finely chopped
 with a handful of fresh parsley
½ tsp. salt, or to taste
freshly ground black pepper
1 egg, lightly beaten

Glaze

2 Tbsp. good Dijon-style mustard
2 Tbsp. honey
1 cup dry white wine and ½ cup water

HONEY MUSTARD CHICKEN
with WILD MUSHROOM STUFFING

Not everyone has a forest for a backyard, but I do, and I am an ardent mushroom gatherer. Wild mushrooms are truly fantastic—earthy and exotic—and when combined with wild rice they easily transport our senses out of any town to a fall day in the woods. Many stores now carry them dried, and though expensive, a little goes far, so if you're not already using them, I hope you'll try. This preparation, similar to the **Pork Roast Provençale**, results in a marvelous stuffed chicken or Cornish hen sumptuous enough for any guest.

Prepare the stuffing by mixing the ingredients. Stuff *chicken or game hens*, gently forcing a piece of bread in last to keep the stuffing from falling out. Place in a roasting pan, sprinkle with *salt, pepper*, and one more teaspoon of *Herbes de Provence*, and roast at 400° for 30 minutes until brown and crusty.

Meanwhile prepare the glaze: mix *mustard* and *honey*. Whisk this gently in a small saucepan with *white wine* and *water*, then pour it over the chicken after the first 30 minutes. Lower heat to 350° and continue basting with pan juices for another 25 minutes (15 minutes for game hens). Remove stuffing to a warm serving bowl, carve chicken or halve the hens and serve in hot pan juices. To thicken the juices, see page 13.

Eggplant Soup Ingredients

    2 medium eggplants
    1 large onion
    2 Tbsp. olive oil or butter
    4 garlic cloves, minced
    a half-inch piece of jalapeño pepper
    a 28-oz. can ground tomatoes
    1 quart chicken broth
    1 bay leaf
    1½ tsp. salt, or to taste
    ½ tsp. ground pepper
    1 Tbsp. *Herbes de Provence*

EGGPLANT SOUP
with HERBES DE PROVENCE

My gratitude to hundreds of *Chocolate Moosse Café* patrons who over the years ordered eggplant soup when it was the last thing they would ever have made for themselves. Judging by the number who asked for the recipe, they weren't sorry! If you like eggplant, you'll like this easy soup:

Finely chop or slice *onion.* Sweat it covered, over low heat in *olive oil* or *butter,* stirring as needed to prevent sticking. Meanwhile, finely dice *eggplants* (half-inch dice are nice) leaving the skin on. If you can make neat dice in your processor, go ahead, but I do this by hand, using a very sharp knife. When the onions are golden brown and very limp, add *eggplant, garlic* minced with *jalapeño* (or *1/4 tsp. red pepper flakes*), *ground tomatoes, chicken broth, a bay leaf, ground pepper,* and *Herbes de Provence.* Bring to boil, lower heat and simmer at least one hour, until eggplant is very soft. Add water or stock to desired thickness. Correct *salt and pepper,* and if it seems too tart for your taste, add a bit of *sugar.*

Strips of roasted red pepper are a fine garnish for this soup, or serve with a dollop of *sour cream* and *chopped parsley or chives,* or grated *parmesan cheese.*

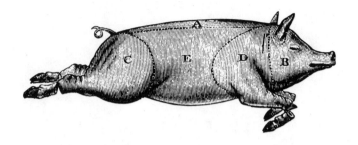

Potée Ingredients

a fresh ham (leg of pork) or other pork roast cut
   —or use a beef roast or stewing chicken
1 cup water or stock and 1 cup white wine or beer
sausages—your choice

Bouillon:
   1 tsp. salt
   ¼ tsp. black pepper
   bone from the roast, if you have it
   1 lb. piece of salt pork, ham, or a ham hock
   2 Tbsp. tomato paste
   2 bay leaves
   4 garlic cloves, minced
   a few flakes of dried red pepper
   2 Tbsp. *Herbes de Provence*
   a cabbage

And for each person:
   ½ carrot
   a small leek
   a baby turnip, or a quarter of a big one
   a chunk or two of peeled celeriac (celery root)
      if available—or use half a stalk of celery

66

POTÉE CHAMPENOISE

There is no way to give the "authentic" version of this dish, my favorite in all the world, because it is only one version of the classic pot of meat and vegetables found in peasant winter kitchens all across Europe and all across time. *Potée*, literally translated, means "a pot of." The word *Champenoise* refers to the Champagne region of France, east of Paris, where I learned to prepare this comforting dish. Every corner of Europe has its potée in some form, all taking advantage of what the cellar had to offer when winter had sealed the fields.

If you think you don't like cabbage, don't give up until you've tried it like this.

The combination of meats can vary. I have seen similar dishes with roast chickens and sausages of all kinds, so try it with what *you* like to eat. In France a piece of salt pork always hung in front of our fireplace. A slice of it found its way into most simmered dishes, but in those days we worked outdoors in the bitter cold and hadn't heard of cholesterol. Today I still use a piece of ham or choose a sausage, then go for a bike ride.

Here's one way to do it: Following the recipe for leg of lamb (page 54), prepare *a fresh ham* (leg of pork). Have it boned and put the bone in with the veggies. If you can't find a ham, use a shoulder or loin. It's a shame to overcook pork, but you should certainly roast it to medium, at 350° about 30 minutes to the pound. Baste with *water* and *white wine* or *beer*.

Meanwhile in a large heavy stock pot, place the bouillon ingredients. *Carrots* are cut lengthwise then quartered; *leeks* are trimmed and carefully cleaned by slitting lengthwise almost to the root and soaking in lukewarm water. Peel, clean, and chunk the *celery root*. Cut *cabbage* in 6 to 8 neat wedges and place in the pot last. Add *water,* or *stock* to not-quite cover, season with *bay leaf, red pepper, Herbes de Provence,* and *salt and pepper.* Bring slowly to the boil and simmer about half an hour until vegetables are tender but not mushy. At the boil, add *sausages* to the pot—*garlic sausage, Polish, Italian, turkey, chicken-apple* —there are endless types.

To serve: There are options. In some traditions the bouillon is drained from the vegetables and served as a first course containing *vermicelles* (tiny noodles). In any case, the meats are sliced and arranged on a platter surrounded by the vegetables, or on a separate platter. Use the pan juices from the roast to drizzle over everything; also use the bouillon to moisten so everything is bathed in juice. The only thing remaining for total bliss is a bowl of tiny *cornichon pickles* and an assortment of great *mustards* and *horseradishes.* This is peasant fare to serve with confidence to the most demanding guest!

SALAD DRESSING for SANDY McIVER

When I prepared a birthday dinner for Bill and Sandy McIver of Matanzas Creek Winery, they gave me a jeroboam of French Beaujolais from Château de la Chaise which had turned to vinegar—I wanted to experiment. A while later I sent them a jar of this salad dressing made from it, which you can make with any fine vinegar:

Mince together in food processor until fine:
   2 garlic cloves
   8 almonds
   ½" piece of ginger

Continue to process this with:

   ½ cup Meaux-type mustard with seeds
   ¼ cup honey
   ¼ cup soy sauce
   ¼ tsp. black pepper
   ¼ cup mayonnaise (optional)
   1 tsp. *Herbes de Provence*
   ¾ cup balsamic or other fine wine vinegar
         (not everyone has an over-the-hill
         grand cru Beaujolais. . .)
   ¾ cup olive oil
   ¾ cup buttermilk

Using buttermilk instead of half the oil in salad dressing has been a great help in keeping down the oil and fats in our diet—and besides, it makes the dressing creamy and delicious. This makes about a quart and keeps nicely in the fridge.

69

Stuffed Vegetables Ingredients

For one large firm cabbage, or 6 total of peppers,
    squash, or large tomatoes, serves six:
  2 cups water with 1 tsp. salt
  1 cup rice

  ½ lb. ground lamb
  ½ lb. ground pork or beef
  ½ cup chopped almonds or pine nuts
  4 diced sun-dried tomatoes
  1 onion, sautéed in butter
  3 garlic cloves
  ½ tsp. ground pepper
  2 Tbsp. *Herbes de Provence*
a handful chopped parsley
  1 tsp. salt
  1 egg
  ¼ tsp. cayenne

  1 Tbsp. tomato paste
  1 cup dry white wine
cherry tomatoes

STUFFED VEGETABLES
with HERBES DE PROVENCE

My Swiss husband Arrigo disdains stuffed peppers and cabbage as *"La Cuisine des Routiers*—Truck Stop Food." While this may be true in Europe, if I found a truck stop in California with good stuffed cabbage I'd stop there any day. At *Little River Café* I made it a personal specialty. We also stuffed large tomatoes, red and green peppers, and various squashes to make a tasty summer medley. It's a bit of work, but worth it.

Cook *rice* in *salted water* until it is still quite firm, about 15 minutes. Let it cool a little, then mix in a bowl with the other stuffing ingredients.

For *cabbage*: Blanch a sturdy cabbage in gently boiling water for 10–15 minutes. Drain, let it cool to the touch, and peel off the leaves. Pairing smaller leaves with larger ones, place some stuffing on each and make neat rolled packages. For *tomatoes, peppers*, and *squashes*: choose short, wide ones. Using a small sharp knife and a spoon, remove the vegetable tops and hollow out the centers. Then gently tuck in the stuffing.

Fit the stuffed vegetables snugly into a well-oiled oven dish. Sprinkle with *salt and pepper*, then distribute *cherry tomatoes* among them. Whisk *tomato paste* into white wine and pour this on. Bake at 350° for about one hour (or microwave 30 minutes at full power). Moisten with more *water* or *stock* to insure their poaching in a bit of juice at all times. Serve hot with cool *sour cream* or *yoghurt.*

Braised Beef Ingredients

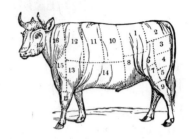

Serves 6

3 pounds trimmed pot roast of beef
    (sirloin tip is best)

Marinade:
    1½ cups dry red wine
    ¼ cup olive oil
    a bay leaf
    1 Tbsp. *Herbes de Provence*
    1 garlic clove, crushed
    half an onion
    6 peppercorns

3 Tbsp. olive oil
20 small boiling onions or one cup chopped onion
¼ cup brandy
2 Tbsp. flour
1 Tbsp. *Herbes de Provence*
2 more cups dry red wine
    (preferably what you'll be drinking)
a bay leaf
¼ tsp. black pepper, or some red pepper flakes
2 Tbsp. tomato paste
2 pounds thick-sliced carrots (about six)
2 more minced garlic cloves

BRAISED BEEF du PÈRE FILLIPOT

On many bitter winter days in France, I took refuge in the house of an old jeweler near the Marne River. Georges Fillipot was a great fisherman and a fine cook, and I will never forget his *Boeuf Carottes*. Beef is disappearing from tables today, but still has an honored place in Western cuisine, as in this hearty braised classic. Red wine and carrots give it a rich sweetness.

Trim and cut the *pot roast* into 2-inch cubes, and marinate overnight. Remove the meat and dry it well, discarding the marinade. Over high heat in a heavy casserole, brown the meat on all sides in *olive oil*. Remove, lower the heat a bit, and in the same pan, brown the *onions*. For an extra-rich sauce, deglaze with *brandy* when they are toasty-brown. Replace the meat, sprinkle with flour and *Herbes de Provence*, stir to coat, and cover with *wine, tomato paste, and seasonings*. Simmer covered for 1½ hours, then add *carrots* and *minced garlic* and simmer (don't boil) for another hour. Add water as needed to keep the meat bathed with liquid.

To finish, add *salt and pepper* to taste, and serve just as is—or to thicken and enrich it, you might purée a *few of the carrots*, adding them back to the sauce. Garnish with *chopped parsley* or *chives*, and serve with boiled potatoes or fresh pasta.

There is good reason to call this comfort food, the world over.

Lapin Les Blank Ingredients

Serves four

1 fat rabbit, 3½ pounds or so,
      (have it cut or do it yourself.)

Marinate overnight in:
  a bottle of dry white wine
  a carrot, sliced
  a sprig of fresh thyme

flour for dusting the rabbit pieces, about 3 Tbsp.
butter and peanut oil, 2 Tbsp. each
salt and black pepper to taste
1 tsp. dried thyme
1 cup reduced chicken stock
1 tsp. *Herbes de Provence*
a bay leaf
2 garlic cloves, minced
a sprig of fresh parsley, and more for garnish
4 large shallots or 1 small sweet red onion
½ cup brandy
juice of ½ juicy lemon
1 egg yolk
2 Tbsp. mustard
½ pint cream (less if you want it leaner)

LAPIN (Rabbit) LES BLANK

Once I had the pleasure of having film maker Les Blank to dinner. Les's films are fascinating portraits of musical and culinary subcultures in America. My husband Arrigo had appeared with his band, *Le Camembert*, playing the hurdy-gurdy in the film *Garlic is as Good as Ten Mothers*, and Les was staying at our house for the weekend. I served rabbit which we munched with pleasure, and when Les asked for the recipe, I wrote it up and called it **Lapin Les Blank**. As a musician and cook, I am crazy about his films, so in tribute to his marvelous work, here's the recipe:

When you're ready to start cooking, take the rabbit pieces out of the marinade and dry them thoroughly. Dust them with *flour* and brown well on all sides in the sizzling mix of *butter* and *peanut oil*. *Salt and pepper* a little and sprinkle with *dried thyme*. Meanwhile, begin reducing the strained marinade in a large heavy pot, bringing it to a gentle boil and adding *stock* if you have some, a *bouillon cube* if you don't; also add *Herbes de Provence*, *bay leaf*, and minced *garlic*. Let it cook down as you brown the rabbit. You may find a good deal of scum forming, so skim it often. Put in a sprig of fresh *thyme* and one of *parsley* to collect scum, and lift them out when the sauce is reduced. Watch the quantity of liquid for your sauce, and add some water if it gets too low.

When the rabbit pieces are well-browned, add them to the sauce and reduce to simmer. Don't boil. In the browning pan, which still contains the fat, put finely chopped *shallots* or *red onion*. Toss to brown slightly, and deglaze with brandy. Add to the simmering rabbit. The addition of the brandy will give the sauce richness and color. There should be enough sauce to almost cover the rabbit pieces, and it should simmer *but not boil* for about 35 minutes, or until tender. The quality of the rabbit will very much determine its tenderness, so try to get a good one.

To finish the sauce, mix together and set aside: the *lemon juice, egg yolk, mustard,* and *cream*. The choice of mustard is yours: a hot-sweet one will give an accent different from that of the more traditional Meaux-style with seeds or Dijon-style. I used a mixture of hot-sweet and Meaux-style. Dilute the cream mixture with a ladle of the hot sauce and add it to the pot. It will turn the whole thing creamy and tangy—and after a few more moments to marry the flavors, it should be ready to serve. *Don't boil it.* Correct for *salt and pepper* and serve garnished with *chopped parsley*. Homemade fettucini— or a good commercial one—would be my favorite thing to swish through all that sauce.

This is a lot of words, but it's really simple. To summarize: 1. Marinate the rabbit, 2. Brown the rabbit, 3. Reduce the marinade, 4. Brown the shallots or onion and deglaze with brandy, 5. Mix egg yolk, lemon, mustard and cream, add to the sauce and serve.

If you can't find a rabbit, use a good chicken.

FRICASSÉE de CHAMPIGNONS
A Mushroom Thing

Here is a tasty treatment for wild chanterelles, boletes, or hedgehog mushrooms. But don't wait for these—use any good mushrooms in your local market. My husband has fixed in his memory a fricassée or stew of mushrooms served in a student bistro near the University in Lausanne, Switzerland. When pressed for his recipe, the old Chef would only say to use three kinds of mushrooms. So if you can, find three.

Cut *one pound of mushrooms* into bite-sized pieces. Sauté on medium-high heat in *3 Tbsp. butter* or *oil* (more if you aren't counting fat), sprinkled with *1/2 tsp. Herbes de Provence*. Toss and stir to sear the mushrooms, not stew them. When they are nutty brown and soft, about ten minutes, deglaze the pan with *2 Tbsp. dry sherry* or *port*. Add *1 clove minced garlic, 1/2 tsp. salt, lots of fresh ground pepper*, and *1/2 cup chicken stock*. Many people like to use more garlic, but I rather err on the light side, to let the mushrooms shine. Stir just to absorb and evaporate the stock, sprinkle generously with *fresh chopped parsley* (very important) and if you like, add *a little heavy cream*.

Use as a side to meat, poultry, or vegetarian main dishes, to stuff omelettes—yum—to mix with rice or toss with pasta, to enrich sauces or pan juices, or on its own.

OTHER DELIGHTS
of HERBES DE PROVENCE

Herbes de Provence are best used in dishes to be cooked at some length, but they are great in some quick preparations, mostly for the grill or barbecue:

To coat *steaks, chops, fish, or chicken* before grilling or broiling, mix *1 Tbsp. of herbs* with *1/4 cup olive oil.* A dash of Worcestershire is an option, too. *Salt and pepper* to your taste.

Try *summer vegetables* tossed in the above mix and grilled or broiled (not too hot) until crisp-brown on the outside and soft in the center. To speed their cooking and relieve congestion on the grill, mix the vegetables with the oil and *herbs*, then prebake 20–25 minutes in a medium oven. You can grill them to sear and finish. Especially good this way are *Japanese eggplant, squashes, and peppers.*

Use *Herbes de Provence* in *lamb stews,* with garlic, vegetables, new potatoes or beans.

Herbes de Provence go wonderfully with *ratatouille,* the classic Provençale stew of eggplant, zucchini, peppers and tomatoes.

Mix with ground beef for the best *hamburgers* ever.

Use to flavor *patés* and *terrines*.

Recipes using

CLOUDS' BLEND HERBS

Basil, Tarragon, Rose Petals, and Dried Red Chilies

DEBRA DAWSON'S

CLOUDS' HERB BLEND
for Seafood, Salads & Sauces

CLOUDS' BLEND
for Superb Seafood, Salads and Sauces

My good friends Penny and G. F. Cloud make and sell marvelous pottery from their shop in Old Town Folsom, California. They were the first to carry my herbs, and had asked for a new blend to feature in their shop. My image of them is a fridge full of basil and a profusion of roses everywhere—on their hand-painted pots and all about the house—so I decided to combine basil and rose petals. The other ingredients just leaped into the bowl.

My customers were asking for a blend for salads, and I had been searching for something wonderful for fish, so it has been a delight to develop this new and delicate mix. I hope you will find your own new ways to use it, and that you will send me your recipes.

Fresh Pasta Ingredients

Serves four

2 cups flour, unbleached or half semolina
2 extra large eggs
1 Tbsp. olive oil
1 Tbsp. *Clouds' Blend Herbs*
a large pinch of salt

Pesto Log Ingredients

a cube of sweet butter (½ cup), softened
¼ cup extra-virgin olive oil
a small handful of fresh basil, finely chopped
1 Tbsp. soy sauce, or salt to your taste
2–4 garlic cloves, pressed or very finely minced

FRESH PASTA "CLOUD 9"

One reason it's so much fun making fresh pasta is that you can flavor it any way you like. My first thought for this lovely fragrant blend was to put it in pasta dough—and yes, it is very nice! Assuming you will be using a pasta machine:

Place *flour* in a mound on a large clean surface, and make a well in the center. In it, place *eggs, oil, salt,* and *Clouds' Blend Herbs* and mix well with a fork. Using the fork, begin incorporating flour from the inner rim of the well, sweeping new flour from the lower part *under* the mixture to keep it from sticking to the board. Mix as much as you can with the fork, then press your (lumpy) dough together with your hands.

Shake what remains loose on the table through a sifter. Discard lumps, and place your ball of dough into the loose sifted flour. Knead by hand, pressing with the palm and folding over the edges, for about 3 minutes, incorporating loose flour. It should be smooth and elastic. Let the dough rest for 5 minutes, then knead and cut by pasta machine instructions. It is very quick and delicious.

For an amusing presentation, make a pesto log. Mix all ingredients, arrange along the edge of a piece of waxed paper, roll snugly and chill until firm. Cut into slices to garnish each portion of fresh **Cloud 9 Pasta.**

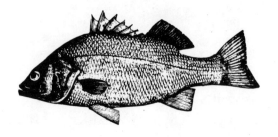

Ling Cod Ingredients

Serves four

2 lb. fresh fillets of ling cod, snapper
    or other firm white fish
½ tsp. salt
fresh ground pepper
1 tsp. *Clouds' Blend Herbs*

Sauce Ingredients

½ cube sweet butter
2 tsp. flour
2 Tbsp. lemon juice
boiling water or fish stock
1 Tbsp. capers
½ tsp. *Clouds' Blend Herbs*

HERB-BAKED LING COD or RED SNAPPER

Preheat oven to 350°. Butter a baking dish and sprinkle with *salt, pepper,* and *Clouds' Blend Herbs.* Place on this *fillets* of uniform size—a third to a half pound per person. Sprinkle another pinch of *herbs* on top of fillets. Bake the fish for 12 minutes for fillets of one inch; test for doneness by flaking with a fork gently at the thickest part. Top with this luscious sauce:

LEMONY BUTTER SAUCE with CAPERS
—*Little River Café* technique

In a small saucepan melt *butter,* then, still on low heat, whisk in *flour,* which will hardly thicken it at all. Add *lemon juice,* and when the sauce curdles, which it will, add *boiling water or stock* by spoonfuls or in a small steady stream, whisking all the while, until the sauce sets and becomes smooth and homogeneous. This requires a steady hand, but is essentially foolproof. The sauce should now be smooth and pale yellow—but stop adding liquid when it's still a bit too thick, as the fish will yield juices in baking which you want to add back to the sauce just before you serve it.

At this point, add *capers* with a bit of their *vinegar, Clouds' Blend Herbs* and *salt and pepper* to taste. Keep pot on very low heat or water bath until the fish is ready, whisk in fish juices and serve with the fillets, garnished with fresh *parsley.* The perfect side dishes are a steamed vegetable and new potatoes or your freshly-made **Cloud 9 Fettucine** (see page 83).

White Wine Fish Chowder Ingredients

a yellow onion, finely chopped and sweated in
2 Tbsp. oil
1 quart fish stock, clam juice, or chicken stock
2 cups dry white wine
1 fish bouillon cube (optional)
a bay leaf
1 Tbsp. *Clouds' Blend Herbs*
1 garlic clove, minced or pressed
¼ tsp. black pepper
salt to taste
2 carrots, finely sliced or diced
2 potatoes, diced fine and neat
      (White Rose are very nice)
1 stalk celery, finely sliced
1 red pepper, julienned
1 pound firm white fish: snapper or ling cod
      (and shell fish as you wish)
Lemony Butter Sauce from previous recipe

WHITE WINE FISH CHOWDER

Make the **Lemony Butter Sauce** as described on page 85. Meanwhile, in a 4-quart saucepan, gently sweat *onion* until limp and golden, add *fish stock, clam juice,* or *chicken stock* with *a fish bouillon cube* (these are hard to find, so when you see them, stock up). Add *white wine, bay leaf, Clouds' Blend Herbs, garlic,* and *black pepper.* Add *carrots, diced potatoes, celery,* and *strips of red pepper.* Bring to a boil and simmer 30 minutes until vegetables are tender. Add the lemony butter sauce, stir and correct for *salt and pepper.*

Cut *fish fillets* into 1-inch pieces, and prepare *shell-fish* as necessary. Five minutes before serving, add these to the simmering soup to just cook through. Serve in warmed bowls with crusty fresh bread for a fine light supper or hearty winter lunch. You can do this when you have leftover fish and sauce—make a small pot of broth and vegetables, then add the sauce and cooked fish at the last minute. It's easy and tasty.

CUCUMBER SALAD
with RASPBERRY VINAIGRETTE

Peel and slice *one large cucumber,* toss it in a strainer with *1/2 tsp. salt,* put on a plate with a weight over it to squeeze out the water. After about an hour, mix the limp cucumber slices with *1/4 cup vinaigrette* (recipe follows), with or without *sour cream.* It took me awhile to get used to the French idea of limp raw cucumbers, but now I love them this way. Of course, the sour cream vinaigrette makes a fine dip for crisp, unsalted slices or any other raw vegetables on the *hors d'oeuvres* tray.

RASPBERRY VINAIGRETTE

Always make more salad dressing than you need at the moment, since it's nice to have extra jars in the fridge. In the food processor or a bowl, whisk together:

1   garlic clove, finely minced or pressed
1   tsp. sweet-hot mustard
½   cup raspberry vinegar
1   Tbsp. soy sauce
1   tsp. sugar
1   Tbsp. *Clouds' Blend Herbs*
½   cup olive or grapeseed oil

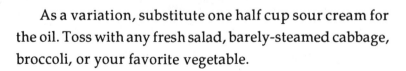

As a variation, substitute one half cup sour cream for the oil. Toss with any fresh salad, barely-steamed cabbage, broccoli, or your favorite vegetable.

POACHED SALMON, NATURALLY

At *Little River Cafe,* our poached salmon was a constant favorite. As with the leg of lamb, it seemed that less was more: salmon doesn't deserve being masked with sauce or over-prepared.

After working on his boat, Jacques would go to the Noyo harbor and choose every fish by feel, since the first secret to good fish is absolute freshness. Here is another:

Prepare a *court bouillon* of *1 cup dry white wine, 1 quart water* or *light fish stock, 1 onion, 1 carrot*—both chopped—*several parsley stems, 1 tsp. sea salt, a sprig of fresh thyme* or *1/2 tsp. dried thyme, 1 bay leaf,* and *6 peppercorns.* Bring to a boil and simmer for 30 minutes.

Strain into a deep flat pan or fish poacher, bring to a boil, and gently add *salmon fillets or steaks of 1/3 to 1/2 pound* per person. Adjust heat to keep it just at the simmer point while the fish poaches, about 7 minutes.

Meanwhile, in a small pan floating in the poacher, melt for each fillet: *3 Tbsp. sweet butter,* with the *juice of 1/2 lemon, 1/2 tsp. Clouds' Blend Herbs,* and some *finely chopped parsley.* When the salmon fillets separate with a fork and have *just* become opaque in the thickest part, remove, drain well, and serve on a warm plate with the lemon-butter sauce. Very simple, very good.

BEET and APPLE PURÉE

During the planning of an autumn wedding dinner, the bride sent me a recipe for a beet and apple purée, which they wanted on the menu. It was so tasty that I will make it again and again. The tarragon accent of *Clouds' Blend Herbs* adds even more sparkle to the tang of raspberry vinegar and the sweetness of the apples.

Trim green from beets, leaving skin on. Wash well, quarter, and cover with salted cold water. Bring to a boil, then simmer about 30 minutes or until tender. Drain and cool, slip off the skins, and chop coarsely.

In a medium saucepan, melt the *butter* and sweat the *onion*, covered, until tender and golden, about 15 minutes. Then add the *apples*, which you have cored, peeled if you like, and chopped. Simmer these with the *sugar, Clouds' Blend Herbs, salt,* and *raspberry vinegar* for 15 minutes, until everything is very tender. Process the apples and beets until very smooth, or pass through a food mill. Return the purée to the saucepan, add *lemon juice* and *salt* to taste, and another pinch of *Clouds' Blend Herbs* if you wish.

This dish is lovely served hot, warm, or cold; it is marvelous with any game or dark meats, sausages, poultry, or fish. In summer, it's a bright and refreshing spot on a salad buffet. Combined with *gelatin*, cooled to set point, then squeezed through a pastry tube, this purée becomes a chic scalloped mound with intense flavor and unusual color.

If you have leftovers, freeze them, or add chicken stock and reheat. Garnish with a little sweet or sour cream, and Voila! Beet and Apple Borscht!

Beet and Apple Purée Ingredients

Serves eight or more

2–3 medium sized beets (about a pound)
1 tsp. salt in water
2–3 Tbsp. sweet butter
a yellow onion, finely chopped
4 tart apples
1 Tbsp. granulated sugar
½ to 1 tsp. salt, to your taste
2 Tbsp. raspberry or balsamic vinegar
juice of a fresh lemon, added to your taste
1 tsp. *Clouds' Blend Herbs*

To mold, add while hottest and stir well:
    1 Tbsp. gelatin dissolved in ¼ cup apple juice.

Dijon-Style Roast Chicken Ingredients

1 large chicken
salt and pepper
1 tsp. *Clouds' Blend Herbs*
half an onion, all one piece
1 more tsp. *Clouds' Blend Herbs*
1 Tbsp. wheat germ
1 cup water, chicken stock or white wine
    and either:
2 Tbsp. Dijon-style mustard
1 tsp. *Clouds' Blend Herbs*
    or:
1 tsp. cornstarch in ¼ cup of cold water
2 Tbsp. mustard
1 tsp. *Clouds' Blend Herbs*
½ cup cream (optional)

DIJONNAISE-STYLE ROAST CHICKEN

Poulet Dijonnaise is a French classic using mustard (Dijon, of course) and, as I learned it, tarragon. It can be rich and complex, or light and easy. Try this:

Sprinkle an oven dish with *salt, pepper,* and *Clouds' Blend Herbs*. Rinse and dry *chicken* and prepare by sprinkling the cavity and surface with more *salt and pepper* and *herbs*. Add the *onion* to the pan. Sprinkle the bird with the *wheat germ* and roast, uncovered, at 350° for 35 minutes until brown and crusty. Pour off fat, baste all at once with *water, stock,* or a mix of *wine and stock*. Cover and continue to roast at 325° for another half hour, basting a few times with pan juices. Remove chicken, cut into portions, and either:

1. Add to the pan juices *2 Tbsp. Dijon-style mustard* and *1 tsp. Clouds' Blend Herbs*. Correct for seasoning and serve directly with chicken in a warmed platter, or:

2. Strain juices into a small saucepan and degrease by blotting surface with a paper towel. If you wish to thicken them a bit, dissolve *cornstarch* in *cold water,* add to the juices, and simmer 5–7 minutes. Add *mustard, Clouds' Blend Herbs,* and if you wish, *cream*. Cream can also be added to the unthickened pan juices. Without the cream, this is a very light sauce with the look and feel of something richer. Mustard and herbs are terrific allies in the search for flavor without fat.

QUICK BROILED CHICKEN

My favorite work-night-in-a-hurry supper is a simple broiled chicken. In the 30 minutes it takes to broil, some rice, potato, or pasta can be prepared, with a vegetable steamed over it in a colander or steamer. With a salad, one half hour to the table!

Quarter a *large fryer*, rinse well with cold water, pat dry, and coat with your favorite *mustard*. Be careful, when handling raw chicken, not to introduce possible bacteria into the mustard pot. Sprinkle with *1 Tbsp. Clouds' Blend Herbs,* and pat some more under the skin as well. Salt and pepper at the table only, as mustard is salty and it may be enough for you.

Set the broiler at a medium-low setting if yours adjusts; if not, you will have to watch for burning and turn the chicken often. Place pieces five inches from the flame, starting the leg-thigh quarters 10 minutes before the breast portions as they take a little longer. Broil together 20–25 minutes more, turning a few times.

They are done when a fork probe produces clear juices. Of course broiling has the advantage of dripping out a lot of fat, while the skin protects the meat from drying. You can then further reduce the fat by removing the skin after cooking, though I confess, I would miss this crispy treat. I like to serve it with more of the *mustard* and little *cornichon pickles*.

Serves four.

CUCUMBERS
Braised in Butter

We are accustomed to crunchy slices of raw cucumber, but we rarely see them in another lovely guise—as a delicate warm accompaniment to fish or poultry. Try them sometime like this:

Peel *two large firm cucumbers*, halve them lengthwise and remove seeds with a teaspoon or melon baller. Cut into either: neat half-inch slices, or: quarter each long half and slice quarters into thick julienne strips. Blanch for 5 minutes in *boiling salted water*, drain and cool 5 minutes in cold water. Drain again thoroughly.

Melt *3 Tbsp. sweet butter* in a saucepan with *1 tsp. Clouds' Blend Herbs* and roll the pieces around in this for two minutes until they are coated. Cover and simmer slowly for 20–30 minutes, until very tender. Moisten with a little chicken or vegetable stock if needed to prevent drying out. Season with *salt, pepper*, another sprinkle of *Clouds' Blend Herbs*, and a splash of *sweet cream*.

Serves four.

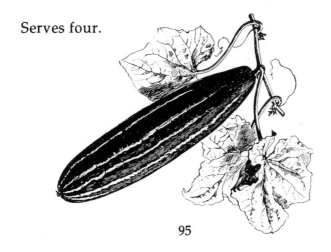

Scallops in Cream Ingredients

⅓ to ½ pound scallops per person, nice and fresh
(The large ones are best, but the little bay scallops
are dandy tossed with pasta.)

2 Tbsp. butter
6 shallots, very finely minced
1 Tbsp. flour
1 cup good fish stock or clam juice
1 cup Extra Dry or Brut Champagne
(If you don't have clam juice, use 2 cups
Champagne with a large fish bouillon cube
dissolved in it.)
a point of cayenne (a careful mound on your knife tip)
1 Tbsp. *Clouds' Blend Herbs*
half a red pepper, cut in thin julienne slices
½ cup heavy cream
salt and pepper to taste

SCALLOPS in CHAMPAGNE CREAM SAUCE

In a wide saucepan on brisk heat, begin reducing *fish stock or clam juice with Champagne* to about one cup. Add the *red pepper* strips to this pot to soften and flavor them.

Meanwhile, gently sauté *shallots* in butter until golden. (If you can't find shallots, use a *red onion*, very finely minced.) Add the *flour* and stir to make a paste, but don't let it brown. Whisk in *fish stock* and *Champagne*, then simmer for five minutes. Keep whisking to prevent sticking and to keep it smooth.

When it is quite thick, add *cayenne, Clouds' Blend Herbs, cream*, and *salt and white pepper* to taste. Return to a gentle boil, and reduce a little more if necessary to make it a bit thicker than you want it, since the *scallops* will yield some juices when they are added. Also remember that if you are going to serve this over rice or pasta, it should be a bit overseasoned to compensate for their blandness.

Rinse *scallops* in cold water, pat dry, and add to the hot sauce. This will of course stop the boil. Stir gently and cook only to heat the scallops through, about 5–6 minutes. Don't boil them, or they'll get tough. Enjoy over linguine, rice, risotto or your fresh homemade noodles, garnished with the *red pepper strips, fresh parsley, tarragon, or chives*. Good for *prawns*, too.

Serves four.

SAUCE BEARNAISE "CLOUD 9"

This is a Bearnaise-style sauce in that it uses vinegar first reduced with herbs, then emulsified and thickened with butter and egg yolks. Not a low-fat choice, it is a rich and luscious special occasion accompaniment to grilled meats or broiled fish, poultry, vegetables, or even tofu. Toss it with pasta or ladle it onto baked potatoes and they become a rich main or side dish. It takes careful attention but is a technique worth learning.

In a small saucepan or double boiler top, combine *vinegar, shallots, Clouds' Blend Herbs*, and *peppercorns*. Bring to a boil and reduce to a few tablespoons. Put in a fine strainer and press out liquid. Return this to the heat and reduce to a syrup of about one tablespoon. Let this cool a few minutes, then add the *egg yolks* one at a time, whisking constantly. Next add *3 Tbsp.* of the *boiling water* which you've prepared in the bottom of the double boiler. Don't stop whisking. Put it back over the hot water, whisk until it's warm and creamy (doesn't take long), then take it off again. Let it cool until you can cradle the pan in your hands, then begin adding the *butter* gradually, beating gently. The *butter* should be at the same temperature as the sauce to incorporate perfectly.

Season with *salt* and *white pepper*, and an additional *pinch of Clouds' Blend Herbs*. If you want a more Hollandaise-like taste, add a squeeze of *fresh lemon*, and enjoy this luscious treat lukewarm—and right away, as it doesn't reheat at all.

The critical moment is when you whisk in the egg yolks. Be sure your vinegar syrup is cooled, and that you add the boiling water gradually, or the yolks will cook and curdle. Otherwise, it's easy.

Sauce Bearnaise Ingredients

½ cup white wine or tarragon vinegar
6 minced shallots
1 Tbsp. *Clouds' Blend Herbs,*
    plus ½ tsp. to finish sauce
½ tsp. crushed white peppercorns (optional)
boiling water
4 egg yolks
½ cup (at least) sweet butter, room temperature
a squeeze of fresh lemon (optional)

QUICK AND EASY USES
for CLOUDS' BLEND HERBS

Toss with green beans or buttered carrots.

Make a new version of herbed cream cheese.

Substitute for *fines herbes* in a cheese omelette.

Add to your favorite salad dressing.

Add to white wine vinegar and steep for two weeks.

Toss with fresh or pickled beets.

Add to butter for dipping fresh asparagus.

Combine with flour and salt to dust fish for sautéing.

Another dip for the vegetable buffet: ***Clouds' Blend Herbs*** with lemon juice and sour cream, salt to taste.

Boil artichokes with lemon juice and ***Clouds' Blend Herbs*** added to the water. Dip in raspberry vinaigrette (page 88) or melted butter with a sprinkle of **herbs**.

Recipes using

HERBS for BEAUTIFUL BEANS

Oregano, Cumin Seed, Thyme, Ground Coriander and Dried Chilies

DEBRA DAWSON'S

HERBS 🌿 FOR

BEAUTIFUL

BEANS

& Mexican Dishes

HERBS FOR BEAUTIFUL BEANS

Beans are a marvel—tasty, economical, low in fat, high in nutrition, and available in a fascinating array of colors, shapes, sizes and flavors.

They can be seasoned in many ways, but I find myself reaching most often for the herbs with a Mexican accent of cumin, oregano, coriander, and peppers. The *Beautiful Beans* blend is a harmonious mixture of these lively flavors, and has become a favorite with my customers. Almost everyone makes and eats beans, especially in the West where the influence of Southwest neighbors is so strong in our regional cuisines. And of course, the *herbs* are useful for sauces, meats, and vegetables as well.

Beans are a staple in vegetarian diets, and should figure in the weekly fare of anyone interested in low fat, high fiber, variety, and great taste. What would we do without them?

Fine Beans Ingredients

3 cups red, kidney, bayo, pinto, speckled, black,
    Anasazi, or even lima or white beans,
    soaked 8 hours or overnight in cold water

approximately 5 cups water or stock
1 cup chopped onion
2 Tbsp. olive oil
1 Tbsp. *Beautiful Beans Herbs*
1 green bell pepper, diced
1 stalk celery, diced or sliced fine
1 or 2 carrots, sliced fine
3 garlic cloves, minced or crushed
a bay leaf
1 tsp. salt, and black pepper to taste
Chilies, as you wish:
    An inch from a serrano, jalapeño, or
    a dried ancho (rusty and shiny) will give
    added fire; an Anaheim (long, green and shiny),
    finely sliced, adds bite and depth, but not too
    much heat.

"A FINE POT of BEANS"

A good natural foods store should offer a heady palette of beans, and many supermarkets are following suit. Beans all respond to the same basic treatment, but each will yield its distinctive character to the result.

To start, it's always a good idea to look through them for stones, discolored beans, and anything else you don't want to eat. Then soak them, and drain.

Sauté *onion* gently in *olive oil* until translucent; stir in the other *vegetables* and *seasonings*, and sweat, covered, for 10–15 minutes. You then have two choices: 1. Add drained *beans*, cover with *water or stock*, and simmer together 1–2 hours until soft; or, 2. cook the *beans* separately with the *stock only* until almost soft, adding the *vegetables* for the last half hour or so. I usually cook them together, which means the flavor of the other vegetables will be leached out into the beans. But you may want the vegetables to retain their own flavor; in that case, add them later.

Use cooked beans in other recipes or eat them straight, garnished with sour cream, cilantro, grated cheese, salsa, chutneys, fresh sweet corn or roasted peppers. Eat them with cornbread or polenta (page 42), baked with *Beautiful Beans Herbs*. Enjoy them often; they're good for you!

SOME VARIATIONS

Black beans are really marvelous, cooked as described on page 105, then accented in some interesting ways:

Their affinity for *celery* is a delight to discover: Increase the *celery* to *4 or 5 stalks,* add *1 tsp. celery seed,* and garnish with the chopped *tiny inner stalks* and *leaves* of the bunch. Swirl in some *fresh* or *sour cream.*

Brazil is credited with another great version: To the almost done beans, add *2 oranges,* peeled, seeded, and chopped, and *1 cup orange juice.* Cuba has contributed another: add *1/2 cup lemon juice or rice vinegar,* and *a cup of cooked white rice.*

Chili—This subject arouses passions among experts. A fine pot of home-style chili can be made with any *red or pinto beans* by adding *a pound of ground beef or pork,* (browned a little first and the fat poured off) and *a 14-oz can of diced tomatoes* for the last half hour. (Otherwise, follow the recipe on previous page.) Use another *Tbsp.* of *Beautiful Beans Herbs,* also *salt* and more *hot peppers* or *cayenne* to taste.

For a new twist to familiar soups, make a fine pot of beans using *lentils or split peas. White and baby lima beans* will welcome the addition of other vegetables as well, more *green* or *red bell peppers, squash, eggplants, tomatoes, or mushrooms.*

A ham bone is always welcome in a pot of beans.

YUMMY COOKED SALSA

Use this lovely salsa/sauce in eggs, burritos, with baked or grilled fish, chicken or meats—anything needing a flavor flash. Or use as the sauce for hearty enchiladas, page 111.

1 large onion, finely chopped
2 Tbsp. olive oil
2 garlic cloves, crushed
1 tsp. salt
1 Tbsp. *Beautiful Beans Herbs*
3 cups fresh chopped tomatoes
    or
a 28-oz. can of crushed tomatoes
approximately ½ cup of water, to desired thickness
¼ cup of red wine

In a heavy medium saucepan, sauté the *onion* gently in *olive oil* until translucent. Add the other ingredients and simmer at least half an hour. If you like *cilantro*, add a fresh and loosely-chopped handful when salsa is hot or cooled.

Refried Beans Ingredients

2 cups raw pinto or red beans,
    soaked in cold water at least 2 hours or overnight
1 Tbsp. *Beautiful Beans Herbs*
½ tsp. salt
3 Tbsp. olive oil
1 yellow onion, finely chopped
3 garlic cloves, crushed
½ green bell pepper, finely chopped
1 Tbsp. *Beautiful Beans Herbs*
more salt to taste
fresh cilantro (optional)

BEAUTIFUL REFRIED BEANS

Refried beans are simple to do, and a natural place to start with Mexican-style cuisine, since they find their way into many other dishes. As their name implies, they can be re-heated again and again—to stuff burritos, tostadas, and enchiladas. Surrounded on a platter by salsas, olives, sour cream and guacamole, they are the basis for a colorful tray of dips for crisp tortilla chips. Wrapped in a tortilla with grated cheese and salsa, quickly warmed in a microwave or stove-top frypan, they will fuel a Little Leaguer through any windy game (spectators too).

Start by soaking beans; drain them and cover with more water, salt, and *Beautiful Beans Herbs*. In a heavy two quart pot, bring to a boil, then simmer for 1½ to 2 hours or until very soft. Drain and mash them smooth.

Meanwhile, sauté the *onion* over low heat in *olive oil*, covered and stirring, until reduced and golden. Add *garlic, green pepper*, and *herbs*; cover and cook another 10 minutes. Mix in the mashed beans, add *salt and pepper* to taste. Add a handful of fresh *cilantro* as well. If you like them hotter, use more *herbs*, chopped *fresh chilies*, dried *chili flakes,* or some *salsa* (page 107).

A spoonful of *Beautiful Beans Herbs* will enrich the flavor of commercial refried beans too, on days when there's no time to start from scratch.

Enchiladas Ingredients

Serves six

corn or peanut oil for frying, about one inch in your pan
12 corn tortillas
3 cups Yummy Salsa sauce (page 107)
>   (Canned enchilada sauce is an option, but add
>   some *Beautiful Beans Herbs* for more flavor)
1 to 2 cups chicken stock, to dilute the sauce as needed

Filling:
> 2 cups refried beans (see recipe on previous page)
>   —or, in a hurry, a 16-oz. can of beans with a
>   spoonful of *Beautiful Beans Herbs*
> 1 pound Sonoma jack cheese, or mild cheddar,
>   or mix the two
> a 16-oz can sliced or diced black olives
> 1 red onion, finely chopped
> 2 cups diced chicken (Use leftovers or simmer
>   a chicken in water to cover and use the stock
>   above. Or use ground or shredded beef, turkey,
>   or pork.)
> chopped fresh cilantro

For vegetarians, sauté two cups of any combination of onions, peppers, eggplant, squashes, and nuts for a tasty meatless alternative. You'll need about 8 cups total of filling. Use vegetable in place of chicken broth.

ENCHILADAS for EVERYONE

Enchiladas come in cheerful red, white, and green; *you* choose the sauce. For the more familiar red ones:

Prepare filling ingredients by dicing or shredding *chicken* or *meats*. Chop the *onions, olives,* or other vegetables you may wish to use, and grate the *cheese*.

Combine in a bowl with *refried beans,* reserving half the *cheese* and half the *olives* for the topping. If you are using *nuts*, chop them into a size you'd want to find in a bite. Combine *salsa* with *chicken stock* and keep warm. If you want it very smooth, purée the salsa before mixing; it should have the consistency of a cream soup.

Heat the *oil,* and using tongs, pass each *tortilla* through it for about ten seconds, enough to sizzle but not to fry crisp. Drain and stack them, then pass each one through the warm *sauce,* and again stack them. Yes, it's a little messy, so have two plates to catch them.

Fill tortillas by placing the filling in a row in the center and rolling snugly. Spread some *sauce* into the bottom of an oven dish, place them seam side down, cover with sauce and remaining *cheese,* and bake or microwave until hot.

Garnish with *sour cream, more chopped olives,* and *fresh cilantro*. With a salad, rice, and fresh corn, a hearty, delicious, and perfectly balanced meal.

ENCHILADAS VERDES

Green enchiladas make use of *tomatillos* instead of red tomatoes. If you aren't familiar with them, they are small plum-sized green orbs with a lacy paper-like husk, which has to be removed. Their flavor is unique: sweet, earthy and tangy.

Make **tomatillo salsa** by substituting tomatillos for tomatoes in the recipe on page 107, then go ahead with your **enchiladas** as on the previous page. You will need to add one step: After removing the lacy husk, plunge the tomatillos into *boiling water* and stir gently for a moment to dissolve the waxy deposit on their skins. There are canned sauces available, which you can enhance by adding a few fresh chopped *tomatillos*, and, of course, a tablespoon of *Beautiful Beans Herbs*.

You may wish to omit the beans and increase the *chicken* for this dish, to highlight the color appeal of the green and white. In this case, use *white cheeses* only.

My friend Elaina Neibel, enchilada expert, swears that garnishing with *crema*, a Mexican *crème fraîche*, is almost as good as having a mariachi band. In place of either, try American *crème fraîche*, or plain sour cream, with cilantro and chopped olives.

ENCHILADAS BLANCAS

White enchiladas, again thanks to Elaina, are made with a *white sauce* and *flour tortillas.* She suggests poaching the *chicken* in *beer* and using *black beans* instead of red. After all, they can't be all white.

Make a white sauce of **4 Tbsp. butter with 4 Tbsp. flour,** whisking in **2 cups milk** and **1 cup of chicken broth.** Add **1 Tbsp. Beautiful Beans Herbs.** Simmer for ten minutes, stirring often. Add *salt* and more *herbs* to taste. Using only *white cheeses,* proceed as described in **Enchiladas,** replacing the red tomato sauce with the white one.

This is an elegant enchilada, maybe a **chinchillada,** so invite your fanciest friends.

Another variation—a little faster to assemble—is to place the tortillas and filling in layers in a casserole. To serve, cut like lasagne.

Red Chili Sauce Ingredients

Makes 4 cups

½ pound (about 30) whole dried New Mexico or
   red ancho chilies (the lustrous rust-colored ones)
water to cover
   or, ½ pound dried New Mexico chili powder
1 lb. Roma or other good ripe tomatoes
one medium onion, finely chopped
2 Tbsp. olive oil
6 garlic cloves, roasted and finely minced
2 Tbsp. *Beautiful Beans Herbs*
1 tsp. salt or more to taste
1–4 Tbsp. sugar; adjust to taste
2 Tbsp. olive or corn oil

RED CHILI SAUCE

This is an exciting sauce with many possible uses. Stem and seed the *chilies* and dry them by shaking in a black iron skillet over a medium flame for five minutes, or in a 250° oven. Don't blacken them. Simmer, covered with water, for 20 minutes, then drain and cool. Meanwhile, roast the *tomatoes* in a skillet or under the broiler. An easy way to roast the *garlic* is with skins on, under the broiler with the tomatoes, for about fifteen minutes, with the flame about five inches away.

Meanwhile, sauté the *onion* in *olive oil*. Put all the ingredients in food processor or blender with *1 cup liquid*—the liquid from the chilies is good if it's not bitter; otherwise use *stock*. Purée to a smooth paste. In a deep pan, heat the remaining oil to the smoke point, and drizzle the paste in carefully, stirring continuously for about five minutes. Add liquid if necessary to obtain the consistency you want, and adjust to taste with a little more *sugar* and/or *salt*.

This sauce is very versatile—use it as a dip for hors d'oeuvres, chips, seafood or grilled oysters, or add to marinades and barbecue sauces. Add it to other tomato-based sauces for added lift; use on meats, chicken, and in bean dishes of all kinds.

Chiles Rellenos Ingredients

Serves six

2 cups **Yummy Salsa** or **Red Chili Sauce**
(pages 107 and 115)
3–4 cups chicken, vegetable, or beef broth,
or more if you want a thinner sauce
12 large chilies: Anaheim, poblano, New Mexico,
ancho—canned ones if you are in a hurry

For a shredded meat filling:
1 pound stewed and cooled pork, beef, chicken,
or turkey, finely shredded with a fork
one medium onion, sautéed in
1 Tbsp. olive or corn oil
2 Tbsp. olive oil
one garlic clove, minced
¼ cup pine nuts
salt and pepper to taste
1 Tbsp. *Beautiful Beans Herbs*

For a cheese filling:
1 pound of jack, fontina, or white cheddar, or mix them
various other fantasies described in the recipe—
keep reading

For the batter:
6 large eggs, separated
½ cup Mexican beer (optional)
½ cup flour. Dust chilies, then beat the
rest into egg yolks.
1 Tbsp. *Beautiful Beans Herbs*
oil for deep frying—canola or corn oil is fine

CHILES RELLENOS

The name Chiles Rellenos (stuffed chilies) applies to a variety of preparations. Here are some ideas which I tried and loved, using *Beautiful Beans Herbs*. It is a bit of work, but worth it.

Start by making **Yummy Salsa** or **Red Chili Sauce**. Dilute the *sauce* or *salsa* with *stock*. For 12 chilies, you need five cups of finished sauce. If you want the sauce perfectly smooth, purée *salsa* first. Taste for salt and pepper, and simmer 15–20 minutes. In a hurry, use a commercial salsa, with *1 Tbsp. Beautiful Beans Herbs*.

Prepare the chilies: Depending on your taste, skills, schedule, and what's available, there are choices: 1. Canned green chilies, drained; 2. Long green *poblano, Anaheim, or New Mexico green chilies*; or 3. Lustrous, brick-red *dried anchos*. If you use fresh green ones, blister them (not too dark) on all sides under the broiler or on a burner, place in a tightly-covered bowl, and ignore for 20 minutes. They will be soft and the darkened parts of the skin will slip off. Don't worry about removing every piece of skin. Carefully cut each chili down the side, avoiding cutting through the stem end, and remove seeds and veins. They are ready to fill.

If you use *dried anchos*, place in a bowl with scalding but not boiling water to soften two hours or more. Drain and slit to remove seeds. Be sure they are soft or the result will be leathery.

Prepare the filling: In your daily cuisine, you might never prepare meats especially to stuff chilies, but left-over meats are a natural filling. For example, prepare a chicken or *pork roast* by poking with slivers of *garlic*, then cover with *water, white wine*, and some *Beautiful Beans Herbs*, bring to boil, and simmer slowly for one hour or until tender. Allow to cool a little in the broth, slice, and serve for supper, reserving about 1 pound for chiles rellenos the next day. The *broth* should be chilled, degreased, and added to **Salsa** or **Red Chili Sauce** as described on previous page.

Shred the reserved *meat* with a fork, and combine with *onion, pine nuts*, and *Beautiful Beans Herbs*. Add *salt and pepper*. Sauté all together in remaining *olive oil*, and carefully stuff peppers with the mixture, rolling them between the fingers to close.

For a cheese filling: Cut *cheese* into sticks of ½ inch by 4 inches long. Lay one stick in each *chili*, and add for variety as you see fit: some *fresh corn*, scraped from the cob and blanched in boiling salted water for 2 minutes; chopped *olives, shrimp, smoked duck, sausage, or a sliver of sun-dried tomato*. Roll them carefully closed, and dust with *flour* mixed with *Beautiful Beans Herbs*.

To make the batter: Separate *eggs*, beat *whites* to firm peaks, set aside, then beat *yolks* until pale and thick. Gradually beat in the *flour* remaining from dusting the chilies (¼ cup apprx.) and the optional beer. Add half the egg whites and mix well. Gently beat in the rest of the whites to make a light batter.

At last, to finish: Heat *oil* in a deep fryer to 375°. Dip *chilies* in *batter* until well coated and fry, removing when golden brown. (A deep pan will work, but for perfect looking chilies, turn them very carefully and only once, spooning hot oil over the uncooked places.) Carefully place into hot **Salsa** or **Red Chili Sauce**, simmer a minute more, then serve immediately on a warm plate in a pool of sauce. For a colorful presentation, pipe a thin lattice of *yellow tomato purée* on each chile and garnish with whole sprigs of fresh cilantro and chopped cold fresh tomatoes.

You may like to try the following variations:

CHILES RELLENOS CASSEROLE

An easier and more foolproof dish, with less fat and essentially the same tastes, is made by following all steps up to frying. Place the dusted stuffed *chilies* in a buttered deep casserole or in individual ramekins, with a spoonful of batter under each, and remaining *batter* spread around and over. Top with some *grated jack cheese*. Bake at 350° for 25–30 minutes, until puffed and golden. Serve **Salsa** or **Red Chili Sauce** on the side.

BLACK BEAN RELLENOS
with BLUE CORNMEAL CRUST

For another treat, sauté *12 strips bacon*, drain off fat and crumble. Add *4 cups mashed cooked black beans*, *2 Tbsp. Beautiful Beans Herbs*, and *salt* to taste. Continue to cook together five minutes. Cool and stuff into *12 chilies*, roll between fingers to close. Beat *6 eggs* till frothy, dip stuffed chilies, roll them in *blue cornmeal*—or yellow if you don't find blue—and deep fry at 375° for about five minutes. Drain on paper towels and serve immediately. Serves 6.

GROUND BEEF, POLENTA
and PUMPKIN SEED RELLENOS

This stuffing makes use of leftover *polenta*, which is often found in my family's fridge. Finely chop *1 large onion*, sweat until limp and golden brown in *2 Tbsp. corn or olive oil*. In processor, chop *1/2 cup toasted pumpkin seeds* for 2 minutes until fine, continue to process with *1 large clove garlic* and *1 Tbsp. Beautiful Beans Herbs*. Add to onions and cook together gently for another two minutes, stirring. Add *1 pound ground beef*, toss briefly to brown and break up, then mix thoroughly in a bowl with *1 cup cooked polenta*, mashed smooth, *1/2 tsp. salt*, and a small handful of *chopped cilantro*. If the mixture is too dry or crumbly to hold together, moisten with *1/2 cup stock or salsa*. Fill chilies as described above, and either dip in batter and fry, or bake in casserole (page 119) 25 minutes at 350°.

GARNET YAM BAKE
with ANAHEIM PEPPERS

Yams are lovely in color and texture, perfect as a background for bright spicy peppers. They are also very nutritious, and indispensable to vegetarians. Try this easy and satisfying combination. Serves six.

Remove tops and seeds from *one red* and *one long green Anaheim pepper*. Blacken them over or under a flame, then cover in a bowl and ignore for fifteen minutes. Scrub *three medium garnet yams* (about three pounds) and remove any blemishes, or peel them completely. Sweet potatoes are fine too. Cut in one-inch chunks. Finely slice *one yellow onion*, and spread into the bottom of a well-buttered baking pan. Remove blackened skin from *peppers*, slice finely, and mix in a bowl with *yams, 1 tsp. salt, and 1 Tbsp. Beautiful Beans Herbs*. Spread over the onions, pour on one cup chicken stock, and bake covered for one hour at 350°. Or microwave at full power for 17 minutes or until soft.

A nutty brown rice pilaf is a fine companion.

For a yummy soup, purée the cooked vegetables, add *4 cups chicken stock*, and some *heavy cream* or milk. Garnish with finely diced red pepper and/or parsley.

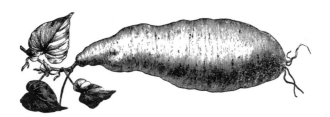

FAST AND EASY EVERYDAY USES
for BEAUTIFUL BEANS HERBS

Beautiful Beans **guacamole**: mash avocados and mix with lime juice, garlic, minced red onion, chopped jalapeños, salt, fresh tomatoes and *Beautiful Beans Herbs*, about a teaspoon per cup of guacamole.

Use instead of your regular chili powder in home-made or canned **chili**.

For **tacos**, add one tablespoon per pound of ground or shredded beef or chicken.

In homemade or commercial **salsa**, add one table-spoon per quart.

Favorite **quesadillas**: sprinkle onto cheese as it melts on a tortilla, top with a slice of fresh tomato and salsa.

Sprinkle on **meats, poultry** or **fish** before broiling, for a pungent Southwest border taste.

Add a tablespoon of *Beautiful Beans Herbs* to your favorite **cornbread** recipe, or to **polenta**.

Recipes using

HERBS for GLORIOUS GOULASHE

Paprika, Caraway, Thyme,
Marjoram, Dill Seed, Dried Red Chilies
and Lemon Peel

DEBRA DAWSON'S

HERBS  FOR

GLORIOUS
GOULASHE

Stews & Slavic Dishes

GLORIOUS GOULASHE HERBS

I once had the pleasure of cooking for a Hungarian Folk Dance camp at the beautiful Mendocino Woodlands, deep in the redwoods. Dancers came from throughout the USA for ten days of intense workshops with teachers from the Hungarian State Ballet and a Hungarian musical ensemble. If you have never seen this graceful and athletic style of dance, by all means try to do so—it's breathtaking! To help make them feel at home, I studied their style of cooking and made an herb blend which featured the flavors so typical of the fiery, glorious goulashe for which Hungarian cooking is famous.

You may find the combination of caraway and paprika a bit unusual at first, but if you experiment with it, as I have, you will find it versatile and provocative in many styles of dish. Paprika experts warn that it should be added *off the fire* lest the high heat caramelize the sugars in a good paprika and ruin the taste.

If there are no Gypsies in your neighborhood, let your imagination supply them as you enjoy some of the following dishes.

Goulashe Ingredients

Serves six to eight

3 medium onions (about 2 cups, chopped)
3 Tbsp. olive oil
a 32-oz jar of gourmet sauerkraut
2–3 lb. trimmed pork—from a shoulder roast, a leg,
      or boneless country style ribs (non–red-meat-
      eaters, use a large roasting chicken)
1 Tbsp. *Glorious Goulashe Herbs*
2 Tbsp. flour
1 tsp. finely chopped garlic
a 14-oz can chicken stock, or about 2 cups
¼ cup tomato purée (about half a 6-oz. can)
½ tsp. caraway seed
1 tsp. salt or to taste
½ cup sour cream and ½ cup heavy cream,
      or all sour cream thinned with a little milk
1 additional tsp. of paprika

SZEKELEY TRANSYLVANIAN GOULASHE

Finely chop *onions* and sweat gently in *olive oil*, covered. (Old recipes call for lard, but few of us would use this now.) In my reading, I've found much ado made of the precise condition of the onions—they must be cooked slowly and at great length to a golden brown paste, caramelized and reduced—so start these first and baby them along. Drain the *sauerkraut* and wash it under running water. You can further reduce the sourness by soaking the sauerkraut in cold water, if you want it quite tamed. Allow it to drain.

Cut the meat into two-inch cubes; if using *chicken,* cut it into portions. When the onions are ready, remove from heat and stir in *chopped garlic, Glorious Goulashe Herbs,* and *flour* to coat onions. Return to heat and whisk in one cup *water* or *stock.* Add the meat, then spread *sauerkraut* over that. Whisk together the *tomato paste* with the remaining *chicken stock* and *seasonings.* Pour this over the meat, and either: 1. simmer tightly covered over low heat for one hour, or 2. bake in 350° oven for one hour. Add a little water if necessary to keep it moist.

To serve: Make the *sour cream* mix. If you add this directly to the pot, it will tie everything together into a tangy, creamy stew, wonderful for a family supper. If presentation is important, serve the Goulashe in a deep heated platter with mounds of *sour cream* on top or on the side. Garnish generously with more *paprika,* and serve with boiled potatoes or egg noodles.

LIPTAUER CHEESE

2 cups cottage cheese (a one pound tub)
2-oz. can anchovies (about 8 fillets)
2 garlic cloves
1 Tbsp. dry mustard
1 tsp. white pepper
4–6 green onions, green part mostly removed
1 tsp. salt
4 Tbsp. *Glorious Goulashe Herbs*
12 oz. natural cream cheese, softened
1 cup (2 cubes) softened sweet butter
1 cup sour cream
¼ cup capers, drained
2 Tbsp. gin (to ripen flavor and add a hint of juniper)

This Hungarian favorite is a nice addition to any buffet table or light summer supper. Beat the *cottage cheese* in a mixer until curds are broken down. In a food processor, mince together to a paste the *anchovies, garlic, green onions, mustard, pepper, salt*, and *Glorious Goulashe Herbs*. Beat the *butter* and *cream cheese* into the *cottage cheese* until smooth but not puréed, then beat in *sour cream, gin, anchovy mixture*, and *capers*. Chill for at least a day, and up to a week. Serve in a glass bowl surrounded with raw vegetables and crackers, for spreading and dipping. It is also delicious on baked or boiled potatoes!

NAPA CABBAGE and RED PEPPER SALAD
with WARM VINAIGRETTE

2 red peppers, stems and seeds removed
4 shallots, finely chopped
1 Tbsp. olive oil or, should you have it, duck fat (!)
½ tsp. *Glorious Goulashe Herbs*
half a large Napa cabbage, finely sliced
another 1 Tbsp. olive oil or duck fat
¼ tsp. salt
3 Tbsp. rice vinegar or good white wine vinegar
1 tsp. sugar

Char the *red peppers* over or under a gas flame until black, place in a covered bowl or wrap in plastic for fifteen minutes. Meanwhile, sauté the *shallots* in *oil* with *herbs* until soft, and set aside. Sauté the sliced *Napa cabbage* in the rest of the *oil* until just wilted, add *salt,* and remove to a colander to drain. Now peel the blackened skin from the *red peppers,* rinse them and pat dry.

Replace the *shallots* in the pan, add the diced *red peppers,* reheat and deglaze with *vinegar* and *sugar.* Add the *cabbage,* toss together and serve immediately. Garnish with another dash of *Glorious Goulashe Herbs.*

PAPRIKA SHRIMP
with GLORIOUS GOULASHE HERBS

Serves three

1 pound medium sized raw shrimp,
   peeled, deveined and patted dry
2 Tbsp. butter or olive oil, or half of each
3 Tbsp. finely chopped shallots
1 garlic clove, minced or pressed
1 tsp. *Glorious Goulashe Herbs*
a little salt and pepper, or a dash of soy sauce
¼ cup dry white wine
⅓ cup sour cream
juice of half a lemon
more paprika to taste
scissored parsley or chives for garnish

Here is a new slant on serving *shrimp*. Heat the
butter or *oil* in a sauté pan, add the *shallots* and toss a
minute, then add *shrimps* and *garlic*. Turn them once
when pink, sprinkle with *herbs* and *salt and pepper*,
continue another three minutes. *Don't overcook!* Remove
them to a heated plate, deglaze the sauté pan with *white
wine* and reduce one minute. Add *sour cream, lemon,*
and *paprika* to taste, return shrimp to sauce and serve
immediately with boiled or steamed rice or pasta. Or
mix right into the rice for a paella-style dish.

EARTHY POTATO-MUSHROOM SOUP

Serves six or more

a large yellow onion, diced or finely sliced
1 Tbsp. each sweet butter and olive oil
1 pound mushrooms, diced
2 pounds white potatoes, diced
1 large garlic clove, minced or crushed
a bay leaf
1 tsp. sea salt, and fresh ground pepper to taste
1 Tbsp. *Glorious Goulashe Herbs*
6 cups chicken stock (or a 49-oz. can)
¼ cup port or sherry
sour cream for garnish

In a heavy 4-quart pot, begin sweating *onion*, covered, in *butter and olive oil*. When onions are golden brown, add *mushrooms*, wild or domestic, and sweat together, covered, until limp. Peel and dice *potatoes*. Add to the pot with *crushed garlic, bay leaf, sea salt, Glorious Goulashe Herbs* and *chicken stock*.

Bring to a boil, lower heat and simmer for 30 minutes until potatoes are soft. Stir to prevent sticking. This soup will have a rich, tawny color from the browned onions, mushrooms and *herbs*. If you wish to enhance it, whisk in *1–2 Tbsp. tomato paste*, or a spoonful of *red chili sauce*, page 115. Add *1/4 cup of sherry* or *port* just before serving, a dollop of *sour cream* in each bowl, and chopped *parsley* or *chives*. Heavenly and earthly!

Braised Chicken Ingredients

Serves four

a 3-pound frying chicken, quartered, or use 4 breasts
4 Tbsp. butter or oil, or half of each
2 medium yellow onions (about 2 cups
      coarsely chopped)
1 tsp. garlic, finely minced
2 Tbsp. *Glorious Goulashe Herbs*
1 Tbsp. tomato paste
2 Tbsp. flour
1½ cups chicken stock
a bay leaf
1 carrot, sliced
½ tsp. salt, and black pepper to taste
1 cup sour cream (optional)

Like most Hungarian-style recipes, this one is not inherently low-fat. But by pouring off the fat after browning the chicken (or by oven-browning with no added fat), and by degreasing carefully at the end, a rich-tasting but lean sauce will result. The sour cream is optional as well, or could be nicely replaced by yogurt or buttermilk.

PAPRIKAS CSIRKE—BRAISED CHICKEN

Rinse *chicken* pieces with cold water and pat dry. Brown well on both sides over medium heat in **2 Tbsp. oil** or *butter*. Use a deep skillet. To save time, begin slowly browning the chopped *onions* in the other **2 Tbsp. oil** in another skillet. When chicken is browned, remove, pour off all fat, and deglaze pan with *1/2 cup chicken stock*. Replace chicken and keep warm.

When the onions are reduced to a soft brown paste, take off the heat and stir in *Glorious Goulashe Herbs* and *minced garlic*. Return to heat, stir in *tomato paste* and *flour* to make a roux, and add the rest of the *chicken stock*, whisking till smooth. Simmer five minutes, then purée in processor if you want a very smooth sauce. Pour this over the *chicken*, adding *carrot, bay leaf, salt and pepper*. Cover and simmer 20 minutes on very low heat.

Carefully place chicken on a serving plate, and keep warm. Degrease the sauce by blotting with a paper towel. Now stir in the *sour cream* and test for seasoning, or serve the sour cream in a cool mound on the side.

Accompany this with wide egg noodles, rice or potato and a crisp green vegetable. Garnish with more paprika and chopped chives.

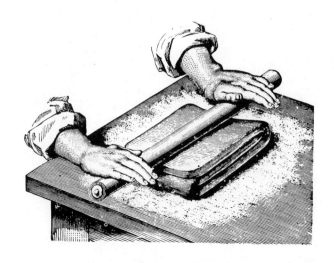

Leek and Cabbage Strudel Ingredients

Serves four as a main course, with eight slices

a small head of cabbage, firm and crisp
3 medium leeks, cleaned and sliced
2 tsp. salt
8 filo leaves, defrosted as package directs
¼ cup butter, melted over hot water
1 Tbsp. olive oil
1 Tbsp. butter
¼ cup fine bread crumbs
1 egg, lightly beaten
¼ cup grated parmesan
¼ cup sour cream
2 tsp. *Glorious Goulashe Herbs*
ground pepper

LEEK and CABBAGE STRUDEL

This is fun on a buffet, as a side to cold cuts or soup, or as a vegetarian main course. Start by grating *cabbage* finely, toss it in a colander with *salt*, and set it aside for at least 15 minutes. Clean *leeks* by slitting around stems to remove outer green parts, leaving tender inner ones and all the whites. Slit lengthwise almost to the root, and soak in lukewarm water to dislodge dirt. Drain and slice finely, then drain again.

Once you know how to do it, *filo dough* is quickly assembled. Lightly flour a work surface or cover with a pastry cloth. Place a *filo sheet* and lightly brush with *melted butter*. (Butter stays liquid if left over hot water, but don't wet the filo.) Lay on another leaf and continue to butter and stack all eight, working quickly to prevent drying. Cover with a barely damp towel while you:

Squeeze *cabbage* to remove excess moisture and salt, then sauté gently in *olive oil* until lightly browned. Set aside. Sauté *leeks* in *butter*, then mix both with *egg*, *parmesan, sour cream, ground pepper* and *herbs*. Taste for seasoning. Sprinkle *bread crumbs* over filo stack, arrange cabbage mix along the long edge in a compact row and roll up snugly. Lay on a baking sheet, cut in half if necessary, or form into a crescent by scoring on the outside edge. It will be easier to slice if the cuts are begun before baking, and you can decorate the roll in this way. Brush with more butter, and bake at 375° for 30 minutes. Serve it warm and flaky, with more sour cream and paprika.

Burgonya Ingredients

Serves six to eight

4 pounds potatoes, peeled and finely sliced
    (about eight medium)
2 Tbsp. butter or olive or canola oil
2 onions, finely sliced or diced
2 Tbsp. *Glorious Goulashe Herbs*
2 medium tomatoes—peeled, seeded, and chopped
1 medium green or red bell pepper, finely chopped
¼ pound each of Stilton, your favorite cheddar,
    Havarti or Dofino, and Gruyère—
      all grated—one pound total
2 crushed garlic cloves
1½ cups chicken stock
1½ cups buttermilk
salt and pepper

BURGONYA—Potatoes Baked
with Four Cheeses and Buttermilk

European cultures have endless variations on oven-baked potatoes, smothering them in white wine, stocks, cream, and cheeses, while accenting with various herbs or spices. In America, our scalloped potatoes are direct descendants of this comforting fare. This version is hearty enough for a vegetarian main course, or perfect to add richness to an otherwise lean entrée. Remember potatoes are rich in fiber and very nourishing.

Preheat oven to 350°. Peel and slice *potatoes* and *onions*, by hand or in processor. If you're in a hurry, parboil the sliced potatoes for 10 minutes. Meanwhile gently sauté the *onions* in oil or butter until limp and golden. Stir in *1 Tbsp. Glorious Goulashe Herbs* to coat onions, then spread in an oven dish with *tomatoes, bell pepper* and *garlic*. Begin layering potatoes with grated *cheeses*, sprinkling each layer with *1/4 tsp. salt, ground black pepper*, and the remaining *1 Tbsp. herbs*. Reserve the *Gruyère* for the top. Add *buttermilk* and *chicken stock*, and bake for 1½ hours if you didn't parboil the potatoes, or ½ hour if you did. Or microwave for about 35 minutes. The long cooking makes everything soft, blended, and luscious.

In Hungary, this would be served with a mound of sour cream or possibly with a sausage. I love this dish with roast beef or any grilled meats in natural juices. And you might try it with other kinds of cheeses, piping hot and garnished with more paprika.

137

Breast of Lamb Ingredients

Serves four

2 pounds breast of lamb, cut between the ribs into
      six or eight pieces
1 tsp. salt
2 Tbsp. olive oil
1 medium onion, finely sliced or diced
2 Tbsp. *Glorious Goulashe Herbs*
2 cups stock or water
one garlic clove, minced
2 carrots, sliced
8 baby turnips, quartered, or 1 large one, julienned,
      (about ½ pound)
a bay leaf
salt and pepper to taste

BREAST of LAMB
with ROOT VEGETABLES

For some people, the smell of lamb is overpowering; for me it's a delight, suggesting sure comfort and warmth after a long day of work. If *you* like lamb stews, here is a rustic, frugal, and delicious winter supper:

Brown the pieces of *lamb* in the *olive oil* and set aside. Pour off all but 1 Tbsp. fat; add *onions* to the skillet and brown gently till limp and golden brown. Sprinkle with *salt* and *Glorious Goulashe Herbs*. Deglaze with *stock* or *water*, replace meat, and add *garlic* and *bay leaf*. Simmer 30 minutes, allow to cool 15 minutes, then carefully remove fat from the surface. Now add the vegetables and simmer, don't boil, for another 30 minutes.

New potatoes can be added to the pot as well, or steamed over it. Your kitchen now has the smell of a European farmhouse, and hungry people may appear from any corner. Serve with big napkins and a smile.

QUICK AND EASY USES for
GLORIOUS GOULASHE HERBS

When making **homemade noodles,** add a teaspoon of **herbs** to each recipe. (See page 82.)

Add a teaspoon per cup of **rice** as it cooks.

Add to dough for **rye bread or rolls.**

Add to **marinades** for basting on grill or barbecue.

Cole slaw and **potato salads** have a new color and accent with *Glorious Goulashe Herbs.*

Simmer with **tomato or onion soups.**

Hummus has a new identity with a spoonful of *Glorious Goulashe Herbs.*

Replaces *Beautiful Beans Herbs* for another fine pot of **beans** (page 105).

Toss with **cucumbers** in sour cream.

Add to **Waldorf** and other apple salads.

Add to creamy **salad dressings** of all types.

MAKE SOME HERB BREAD

Herb Bread Ingredients

5 cups flour plus one more cup to add as needed
  (try 3 cups unbleached to 2 cups of whole wheat,
  rye or buckwheat)
2 cups water (or half milk)—warmer than lukewarm
1 Tbsp. instant yeast or 1 pkg. dry yeast
1 Tbsp. salt (less if you wish)
2 Tbsp. honey
2 Tbsp. oil
1 Tbsp. *Good Thyme Herb Blend*, your choice

Abbreviated recipe: Mix everything, knead until smooth and elastic, rise twice, form two loaves, glaze with a beaten egg, bake 35–40 minutes at 375° until hollow and crusty.

MAKE SOME HERB BREAD

I make bread constantly, especially since I discovered that both my heavy duty mixer and food processor will do it with so little trouble. In our restaurant days, we mixed every bit by hand; I still do it often and recommend this for body and spirit. The dough can be mixed, kneaded, risen, and punched down all in the same large bowl. Likewise, it never has to leave the bowl of your processor or mixer until time to form into loaves.

There are many combinations of *flour, seeds, oil, milk, sour* and *yeast starters,* but the one to remember for simple everyday use is **the starting dry-to-liquid ratio: five to two.** This is what my mixer bowl will handle, and it makes two loaves. Depending on the humidity, you will have to add another cup or more of flour, and knead it in to get a smooth, elastic dough, but that is fine. It is easier to start out too wet and add flour than the contrary. I wish everyone knew how forgiving bread dough really is—if you don't kill the yeast by liquid too hot or too cold, and you don't let the dough rise too long to where the yeast gets "tired" and lets the dough fall, you will certainly end up with bread. Just how perfect the result is, is a matter of some practice and sometimes luck, but try this simple everyday bread, and if you're not already a confirmed baker, you might become one.

For variety, add a tablespoon or two of any *Good Thyme Herbs* to the dry ingredients, depending on the flavors of the food it will accompany. I love to bite into a fennel or cumin seed, or to find a trace of curry in my grilled cheese sandwich. Bread looks, smells, and tastes great with the addition of herbs.

This can all be done easily by hand as well, and is, so I'm told, good for the bust. For the restaurant, we would knead a five pound batch of flour at once in a big stainless bowl, and yes, that is *really* good for the bust. Half of that, 8 cups, is quite manageable, and 5 cups, as I suggest here, is hardly even a workout.

For everyday use, I have found it practical to go to my local bakery and buy a one pound package of an instant yeast called **Saf Instant**. It comes vacuum packed and is the easiest yeast imaginable. You just mix it with the dry ingredients—no proofing, no mixing on the side. It keeps forever in a glass jar in the fridge, and really helps to make breadmaking easy and routine. So use *1 Tbsp.* of this *instant yeast* per 5-cup batch or *1 cake* or *1 package of regular yeast*, dissolved as directed, and added as a part of the liquid ingredients.

IN THE MIXER OR BY HAND

Start with *5 cups of flour*, combined as you like, or for French bread, all white unbleached. I usually combine *3 cups unbleached* to 2 of *whole wheat, rye* or *buckwheat*. For a lighter bread with a little whole wheat texture and color, use 4 cups unbleached to one of whole wheat. Another cup should be on hand to adjust texture.

When using the dough hook, mix the dry ingredients well. A little handful of finely cut 7-grain cereal or wheat germ at this point will also add texture and nutrients. Dissolve *salt*, *honey* and *oil* in *warm water* (warmer than lukewarm, since the flour will cool it). You can also use half milk for a richer bread. If you dissolve your yeast, make sure to use a total of two cups liquid. Add *1–3 Tbsp.* of any of the *herb blends*.

Add the liquid to the mixing bowl, and—on low speed—allow the dough hook to combine everything, then to knead the dough for about five minutes. You may need to push the dough toward the center with a spatula at first, and if it's too sticky to touch when well mixed, begin adding the sixth cup of flour until the dough is smooth and elastic. You can knead it some more by hand, if you wish, on a floured board.

Cover with a damp towel and leave it right there if it's warm; if not, move to a warm place (gas oven with pilot light is optimal). In an hour, turn on the dough hook again and let it punch down and knead for another minute. An hour later, turn the dough out on a floured board, knead a minute and form two loaves. Brush loaves with egg white beaten with a little water and place them in oiled loaf pans or on a flat sheet sprinkled with coarse cornmeal. Let them rise another half hour while you preheat the oven to 375°. Bake for 30–40 minutes, depending on the shape of the loaves. When they're browned, crisp, and sound hollow when you tap, you've got bread!

IN THE FOOD PROCESSOR:

Your food processor will be quite comfortable with the same ingredients.

Using the short-bladed plastic pastry blade, let it mix everything until the dough forms a ball in the bowl, then continue for about a half a minute, letting the ball whirl around the stem. If the motor bogs down, or the dough is too sticky, add the sixth cup of flour a quarter cup at a time. The instruction books for my processor say it can make a dough of 7 cups of flour, but in my experience, this is too much if I want to leave it in the bowl to knead and rise. This is truly lazy bread. You can mix more if you want to turn it out on the board and knead it by hand.

After the dough has risen in the bowl, blade and all, for one hour, punch it down and knead it a bit more by processing for 15 seconds. One hour later, do it again, turn onto a floured board to form two baguettes or loaves, and bake as described on the preceding page.

I hope that by being so casual about technique and combinations of ingredients, I have convinced you how easy it is. Once you know how dough acts, you will never need a recipe again. Using the mixer or food processor, you can spend ten minutes at breakfast, have hot bread for lunch, and that great smell for the rest of the day!

Fresh bread can change your whole day, and good food can change your life. **Keep on cooking!**